Student-to-Student Sexual Harassment K–12

Strategies and Solutions for Educators to Use in the Classroom, School, and Community

Bernice Resnick Sandler
Harriett M. Stonehill

Rowman & Littlefield Education
Lanham, Maryland • Toronto • Oxford
2005

Published in the United States of America
by Rowman & Littlefield Education
A Division of Rowman & Littlefield Publishers, Inc.
A wholly owned subsidary of The Rowman & Littlefield Publishing
Group, Inc.
4501 Forbes Boulevard, Suite 200, Lanham, Maryland 20706
www.rowmaneducation.com

PO Box 317
Oxford
OX2 9RU, UK

British Library Cataloguing in Publication Information Available

Library of Congress Cataloging-in-Publication Data

Sandler, Bernice Resnick.
  Student-to-student sexual harassment, K–12 : strategies and solutions for
educators to use in the classroom, school, and community / Bernice Sandler,
Harriett M. Stonehill.
    p. cm.
  Includes bibliographical references and index.
  ISBN 1-57886-261-2 (pbk. : alk. paper)
  1. Sexual harassment in education—United States—Prevention—
Handbooks, manuals, etc. I. Stonehill, Harriett M., 1930– II. Title.

LC212.82.S28 2005
371.5'8—dc22
                                                        2005001996

To all students: May you have a safe learning environment free of sexual harassment, to grow and develop.

Contents

Preface

Georgie Porgie, pudding and pie
Kissed the girls and made them cry

What's happening here?

Why did the girls cry?

Is Georgie Porgie a sexual harasser?

Was Georgie Porgie's behavior uninvited and unwanted physical contact?

Should the girls tell Georgie Porgie to stop? Will he stop?

Should the teacher who saw the incident do anything?

Should the girls tell someone, such as their teacher or principal?

If so, how should the adult respond?

Do the girls feel safe in school?

What else might Georgie Porgie do if no one stops his behavior?

How will his behavior, if it is allowed to continue, affect his own personal future and choices? How will it affect his social development and school achievement?

When Georgie Porgie grows up, what kind of adult will he be? What kind of employee and coworker? What kind of parent? What kind of neighbor? What kind of citizen?

How Georgie Porgie turns out may well be related to how his school, family, and community respond to his behavior.

har-ass, transitive verb. **1.** To disturb or irritate persistently. **2.** To wear out; exhaust.

Synonyms: aggravate, agitate, anger, annoy, antagonize, badger, bait, bedevil, belittle, bother, deride, denigrate, distress, disturb, enrage, exasperate, frustrate, gall, goad, grate, humiliate, incense, infuriate, insult, irk, irritate, heckle, inflame, jeer, madden, miff, mock, molest, nettle, offend, peeve, perturb, pester, plague, provoke, rankle, ridicule, rile, sneer, taunt, tease, torment, upset, vex.

More than ever, schools are concerned about safety and violence. Unfortunately, schools often overlook a common reason why many students feel unsafe in school—they are sexually harassed by other students. Indeed, students are sexually harassed more often by their peers than by adults. Studies show that 50–90 percent of girls *and* boys experience student-to-student harassment. These behaviors make them feel unsafe, isolated, and anxious, lowering their self-esteem and inhibiting their ability to learn. Sexual harassment incidents have been increasing during the past few years. Incidents are also increasing at an even higher rate in the lower grades. Peer-to-peer student sexual harassment is a serious problem with serious emotional, educational, and developmental consequences.

This book, *Student-to-Student Sexual Harassment K–12: Strategies and Solutions for Educators to Use in the Classroom, School, and Community*, offers solutions, strategies, and procedures to deal with the growing problems of sexual harassment in schools.

We, the authors, have careers that provide us with opportunities to talk directly with teachers, administrators, families, attorneys, and policy makers. These discussions have led us to conclude that schools need workable solutions, specific strategies, and guidelines to change the present situation. It is through such measures that students can feel safe to learn and develop. Effective procedures will result in fewer incidents and healthier relationships among students.

It is critical for schools to recognize the importance of dealing with student-to-student harassment as a major educational, social, and legal problem and to:

• Develop specific policies and procedures to be implemented at every level

- Introduce new programs and techniques into the school environment and curriculum that encourage respectful relationships among students
- Involve participation of families, community leaders, and local organizations in creating a sexual harassment–free environment

Schools need detailed, pragmatic strategies on how to respond to sexual harassment when incidents occur and how to do the following:

- Establish protocols to address sexual harassment incidents
- Provide specific procedures to address incidents in terms of the harasser, the harassed student, staff, family, and community
- Delineate consequences and follow-up activities
- Reevaluate educational programs, training, dissemination, and increased safety procedures when necessary

This comprehensive book will enable schools to:

- Assess the extent of sexual harassment
- Build effective policies and procedures
- Design training programs for staff, including how staff should respond and intervene when sexual harassment occurs
- Design educational programs for students
- Develop outreach programs for families and community
- Create a school and classroom environment where sexual harassment is less likely to occur
- Provide extensive resources

Additionally, the authors' knowledge of how change can best occur includes techniques to gain the cooperation and involvement of families, community leaders, and local organizations. It is only through the full collaboration of the district, the school and all its entities, the families, and the community organizations that individual students can begin to feel safe at school and then be able to learn. Only by feeling safe and free of sexual harassment can students invest their energies into learning and participating in school and community clubs and activities.

All of the incidents described in this book are real.

CHAPTER 1

An Overview of Student-to-Student Sexual Harassment

A ten-year-old girl in a Tennessee elementary school was repeatedly harassed by two eleven-year-old boys who attempted to rape and assault her. They threw her to the ground and fondled her breast, buttocks, and genitals, asked her if she was a virgin and told her they wanted to have sex with her. The girl stated in court that this happened twenty to thirty times. The girl once passed a note to her teacher who tore it up and told her not to tattle. The girl missed school, her grades dropped, and she could not finish her work.[1]

This section provides a brief overview of student-to-student sexual harassment. These topics are discussed in greater detail in the chapters that follow:

What Is It?
Is It Illegal?
How Often Does It Occur?
Who Does the Harassing?
Who Gets Harassed?
When Does It Start?
Where Does It Happen?
Should Schools Take Sexual Harassment Seriously?
Girls Get Harassed
Boys Get Harassed Too
Gay, Lesbian, and Bisexual Students Also Experience Harassment
Disabled Girls Are Also at Risk

WHAT IS IT?

Sexual harassment is any behavior of a sexual nature that is unwanted and unwelcome. It can be saying something sexual to someone, putting sexual pictures in someone's locker, leering, or touching someone in a sexual way. The essential fact is that the student does not want or welcome this sexually related behavior.

IS IT ILLEGAL?

Schools can violate federal and state statutes when they ignore sexual harassment.

HOW OFTEN DOES IT OCCUR?

In the United States, student-to-student harassment is the most common form of harassment faced by students; indeed, students are more likely to be *sexually harassed* by other students than they are to be *bullied*. Thirty percent of students are involved in traditional bullying as victims, bullies, or both.[2]

In contrast, approximately four out of five students or 80 percent are sexually harassed by their peers, with some studies reporting even higher figures. Data reveal the following:

- Six in ten students experience it often or occasionally.[3]
- Fifty-seven percent of girls and 42 percent of boys have been touched, grabbed, or pinched in a sexual way.[4]
- For African American girls the figures are even higher: 67 percent have been touched, grabbed, or pinched in a sexual manner.[5]
- Fifteen percent of white girls, 18 percent of Hispanic girls, and 28 percent of African American girls have been forced to kiss someone.[6]
- Gay, lesbian, and bisexual students have the highest rate of harassment. They experience an *average of twenty-five incidents per day*.[7]
- Peer harassment occurs least frequently in primary school, more often in middle and high school.

- Although there is a general consensus that sexual harassment in the workplace may be decreasing, student-to-student sexual harassment may be *increasing* in elementary and secondary schools.
- One in ten students is estimated to have been the victim of teacher or staff sexual misconduct.[8]

WHO DOES THE HARASSING?

Both boys and girls harass. In addition to boys and girls sexually harassing each other, boys sometimes harass boys, and girls harass girls. Boys are more likely than girls to harass other students: about 57 percent of boys admit to sexually harassing someone. About half of girls admit to harassing someone.[9]

WHO GETS HARASSED?

Both boys and girls are harassed. About 79 percent of boys and 83 percent of girls report having been sexually harassed physically and/or verbally.[10] Girls not only experience more kinds of harassment more often but were also more upset by the incidents than boys.[11]

WHEN DOES IT START?

Thirty-three percent of high school students said that they first experienced sexual harassment in sixth grade or earlier.[12]

WHERE DOES IT HAPPEN?

School sexual harassment occurs most often in public places such as hallways, classrooms, cafeterias, school buses, bathrooms, the schoolyard, and on school trips.[13] Usually other students and/or school personnel are around when it happens.

SHOULD SCHOOLS TAKE SEXUAL HARASSMENT SERIOUSLY?

Sexual harassment can get in the way of students' learning. Therefore, teachers and administrators must take reports of sexual harassment very seriously and take action to stop the harassment. Increasingly schools are responding to incidents of student-to-student harassment, although in a number of schools, sexual harassment is often ignored, unlike other antisocial acts such as vandalism, theft, disobedience, cheating, and truancy. Too often children are forced to tolerate all sorts of harassing behaviors, including sexual assault and abuse—behaviors that are not tolerated when they happen to adults. Sometimes school personnel believe that sexually harassing behavior is a transient problem and therefore it does not receive serious attention.

GIRLS GET HARASSED

- I walked down the hall today while some moronic guy whistled and said "Nice breasts, baby." (tenth-grade girl)
- I guess a look. . . . He was staring down my shirt and it made me feel uncomfortable. (tenth-grade girl)
- A guy slapped my butt when walking down a crowded hall. (student not identified)
- At lunch, a couple of boys at my table started talking about my dog and how they think I have sex with my dog. The longer they talked the nastier they got. (eleventh-grade girl)
- Being forced to kiss someone. (ninth-grade girl)
- Someone made a motion like they were masturbating. (eighth-grade girl)[14]

BOYS GET HARASSED TOO

- A girl pulled down my shorts, exposing my boxers, and then kissed me. (eighth-grade boy)
- Girls hug me without me wanting to occasionally. (eighth-grade boy)
- This girl grabbed my penis. (tenth-grade boy)

- Some idiot jocks called me gay. . . . They use that as a generic slam for anyone that's different. (tenth-grade boy)
- A girl smacked my butt. (ninth-grade boy)
- An attempt to kiss me . . . it was unwanted and I made that clear. (eleventh grade boy)[15]

GAY, LESBIAN, AND BISEXUAL STUDENTS ALSO EXPERIENCE HARASSMENT

A gay, lesbian, or bisexual high school student hears an average of twenty-five anti-gay epithets a day. Teachers who hear these slurs fail to respond to them 97 percent of the time.[16]

- The gay student had been beaten to the point of requiring surgery to stop internal bleeding, was urinated on and spat upon, and was victimized when two students held the boy to the ground and performed a "mock rape" on him, saying that he should enjoy it.[17]
- Through her sophomore year at a suburban Virginia high school, the seventeen-year-old girl endured taunts of "dyke," graffiti in bathrooms, and book bags thrown at her. "It was so painful to walk between my classes," said the openly gay student. "There's a lot of self-respect going down the drain. . . . You're like 'Yeah, I'm a horrible person.'"[18]
- The gay student was walking in the school parking lot to the building when the boys called him a "faggot." When he walked into the building, they jumped him: "I remember being kicked in the face. They were screaming 'You [expletive] faggot' while they were hitting me." About a week later, friends of the attackers chased him home with a baseball bat. Not long afterward, he swallowed two vials of sleeping pills and antidepressants. "I thought, 'Before someone kills me, I'm gonna kill myself.'"[19]

DISABLED GIRLS ARE ALSO AT RISK

School officials may view disabled girls as unattractive or as asexual and may have difficulty believing that anyone harassed them, or because of the nature of their disability, believe that these girls are not able to report accurately.[20]

A twelve-year-old special education student was sexually assaulted by three boys in her Washington, DC, school basement. When she reported the incident, the principal spoke to the children involved, but did not believe the girl's report and did not inform the girl's parents about what happened. The police learned about the incident through other sources and the three boys were arrested. They were suspended for ten days and then returned to school. The incident was well-known among other children in the school who then began to ridicule the girl. The mother repeatedly asked for her daughter to be transferred to another school, but to no avail. When the incident was reported in the newspaper, the child was finally transferred.[21]

NOTES

1. "Supreme Court's Teacher-Student Ruling Is Applied to Student-to-Student Harassment," *Educators Guide to Controlling Sexual Harassment*, Monthly Bulletin, October 1998, p. 4.

2. S. Okie, "Survey: 30% of U.S. School Children Involved in Bullying," *Washington Post*, April 25, 2001, p. A12.

3. *Hostile Hallways: Bullying, Teasing and Sexual Harassment in School* (Washington, D.C.: American Association of University Women, Educational Foundation, 2001), p. 4.

4. *Hostile Hallways*, p. 23.

5. *Hostile Hallways*, p. 24.

6. *Hostile Hallways*, pp. 24, 25.

7. Data reported by the Gay, Lesbian, and Straight Education Network (GLSEN), *Young and Gay, Educator's Guide to Controlling Sexual Harassment*, Monthly Bulletin (December 1999), p. 13.

8. C. Shakeshaft, *Educator Sexual Misconduct: A Synthesis of Existing Literature*, U.S. Department of Education. Retrieved July 22, 2004, from www.ed.gov/rschstat/research/pubs/misconductreview/report.pdf. Shakeshaft's estimate is based on an extensive analysis of research, newspaper and media sources, child sexual abuse data, practice-based first- or third-person descriptions, and other information.

9. *Hostile Hallways*, p. 40.

10. *Hostile Hallways*, p. 4.

11. *Hostile Hallways*, p. 32.

12. *Hostile Hallways*, p. 25.

13. *Hostile Hallways*, p. 28.

14. Response to the question, "What was your most recent experience with sexual harassment?" *Hostile Hallways*, p. 24.

15. *Hostile Hallways*, p. 24.

16. Data reported by the GLSEN in *Young and Gay*, p. 13.

17. *Nabozny v. Podlesny*, 92 F3d 446 (7th Cir. 1996).

18. L. H. Sun, "As Gay Students Come Out, Abuse Comes In," *Washington Post*, July 20, 1998, pp. A1.A.

19. Sun, "As Gay Students Come Out, Abuse Comes In," A1.

20. H. Rousso, "Young Women with Disabilities," *NCSEE* [National Coalition for Sex Equity in Education] *News* 4 (1998–1989): 19–20.

21. S. Horwitz, "D.C. Student to Transfer after Reports of Sexual Assault," *Washington Post*, January 12, 1992.

CHAPTER 2

Why Schools Must Be Concerned about Sexual Harassment

Use these sections to understand what sexual harassment is and the behaviors exhibited by both harassers and victims:

Examples of Sexually Harassing Behavior
What Is Sexual Harassment?
What Kinds of Behavior Are Considered to Be Sexual Harassment?
Is Sexual Harassment Illegal?
Why Does Sexual Harassment Happen?
Sexual Harassment Affects All Students
Why Students Don't Report Sexual Harassment
Where Does Sexual Harassment Frequently Occur?
Ten Myths about Student-to-Student Sexual Harassment

EXAMPLES OF SEXUALLY HARASSING BEHAVIOR

- When she entered middle school, boys in her class called her names, such as "whore" "dog-faced," and "ugly." They often shoved her, snapped her bra, and spat on her. The child's reaction: "By the end of each day when I got home, I usually cried. I never wanted to go to school, I hated it so much." Her grades dropped from As to Bs. Complaints to the school did not stop the harassment. One teacher told her that people would call her names all her life and she would have to deal with it. Her parents pulled her out of the school in midyear, enrolling her in a private school, and later filed a lawsuit against the school.[1]

- "Today, as usual, I observed sexist behavior in my art class. Boys taunting girls and girls taunting boys has become a real problem. I wish they would all stop yelling at each other so that for once I could have art class in peace. This is my daily list of words I heard today that could be taken as sexual harassment: bitch, hooker, pimp, whore."[2]
- Every day for many months, when the girl went to school she was surrounded by a group of boys who called her "a cow," an illusion to her large breasts, and would make "mooing" sounds to her. Sometimes they would follow her around, saying the same things again and again.[3]
- Both boys and girls compile "slam books" that name and rate students in negative sexual terms such as "biggest slut," "worst in bed," "ugliest girl," or "biggest prude." Girls are often called "whore" or "slut," and boys are often called "faggot" or "condom seller."[4]

Sexual harassment is unacceptable. It is unacceptable in the workplace, and it is unacceptable in school. Students should not fear for their lives or safety on school grounds, nor should they be in fear of being bullied or harassed.[5]

WHAT IS SEXUAL HARASSMENT?

Sexual harassment is any form of *unwanted sexual behavior* that makes students feel uncomfortable and unsafe, so that they are often unable to focus on learning, studying, working, achieving, or participating in school activities. Sexual harassment includes sexual assault and abuse, which are on the same continuum. It is a form of bullying, where one student attempts to intimidate another student by using sexuality as a weapon. This unwelcome behavior is verbal, physical, or both, and occurs between boys and girls and between students of the same gender. Sometimes it involves a group of students harassing others. It also includes harassment of lesbian and gay students.

Although teachers, students, and parents typically recognize bullying behavior, they are less likely to recognize or acknowledge peer sexual harassment. Many adults fail to recognize this behavior as sexual harassment when it occurs among students. Student-to-student sexual harassment is prohibited under law; bullying is not. Although some schools offer "bullying prevention programs," they often fail to include sexual harassment as a form of bullying.

WHAT KINDS OF BEHAVIOR ARE CONSIDERED TO BE SEXUAL HARASSMENT?

Sexual harassment covers a wide range of behaviors such as the following:

- Sexual intimidation by word or action
- Sexualized insults and name-calling, such as calling girls "sluts," "whores," "cows," "pussies," or "lesbians," or calling boys "fags" and "pussies"
- Sexual graffiti in places such as bathrooms, cafeterias, hallways, stairwells, on desks and tables, on lockers, and in outdoor areas
- Pictures or displays of sexually suggestive objects, or other materials
- Suggestive cartoons, pornography
- Pulling down a student's pants, flipping up skirts, or snapping bras
- Sexualized remarks or off-color jokes
- Circulating lists describing alleged sexual attributes or activities of students
- Spreading sexual rumors about students
- Unwanted phone calls, e-mail, regular mail, or notes about sexuality or that are obscene and/or threatening
- Pressure for sexual activity
- Teasing about a student's sexual activities or lack of sexual activity (Note: teasing can sometimes be a form of affectionate play between individuals but it can also be a form of humiliation and intimidation.)
- Offensive touching and groping, including breast, crotch, penis, or buttocks grabbing, and rubbing against a student's body
- Sexual assault, abuse or rape
- Masturbating or touching of one's genitals or simulating intercourse

When behaviors have names, it means that the behaviors are happening often. Names for sexually harassing behavior may vary from place to place:

- "Spiking" or "pantsing"—pulling down someone's pants, shorts, or skirt. This happens more often to children wearing clothing that has an elastic band in the waist. (Some children refuse to wear that kind of clothing because of fear of having it pulled down.)
- "Snuggies," "wedgies," "Melvin," "wet willies," "rear admiral"—pulling up someone's underwear from the back so that it goes in between the buttocks. In some instances children have been hung from a hook or post by the pulled-up underwear.
- "Goosing"—grabbing someone's genitals, usually from behind, and done quickly.
- "Slam books"—books in which students' names are listed along with derogatory comments, usually with a sexual focus. The comments may be passed from one student to another, distributed by e-mail, or posted on a website.

Sexual harassment and bullying are unwanted behaviors by their victims. Both involve a difference in power—the power of one peer over another. Boys often have more physical power than girls; a group of harassers is more powerful than its single target; popular students have more social power than others. These differences in power are exhibited in boy/girl, girl/boy, boy/boy, and girl/girl sexual harassment.

Although not all bullying is sexual harassment, most sexual harassment is a form of bullying. Both bullying and sexual harassment intimidate, both are a form of aggression, and both have the potential to harm both the victim and the person committing the aggression.

Letter to Dear Abby

Dear Abby:
I'm an eleventh-grade girl. Our student handbook states that "public display of affection is discouraged and could result in a disciplinary action." If this is true, shouldn't a student also get into trouble for sexual harassment?

A guy in one of my classes has been touching, grabbing and pinching me. I told some of my girlfriends, and two of them said he does the same thing to them. We hadn't wanted to tell each other but now we're glad we did.

We went to the assistant principal's office with our complaint. He gave the boy one day of detention. After that, things got worse. The creep is still picking on us, and our school isn't doing anything to make him stop.

What do we do now, Abby? Were we wrong to tell? If not, how come nobody is doing anything to protect us? School is supposed to be a safe place, right?

Please help us.

Three Girls from Zanesville, Ohio[6]

IS SEXUAL HARASSMENT ILLEGAL?

Not only is student-to-student harassment painful and an impediment to student learning and development, it is prohibited by several laws and regulations:

- Title IX of the Education Amendments of 1972 prohibits sex discrimination in schools receiving federal dollars. Under Title IX schools can be held liable for monetary damages *if* they know that sexual harassment exists *and if* they are "deliberately indifferent" to it *and* the harassment is so severe, pervasive, and objectively offensive that it effectively affects the student's access to an educational opportunity or benefit. (In *Davis v. Monroe County Board of Education*, the U.S. Supreme Court confirmed that Title IX's prohibition of sex discrimination includes student-to-student sexual harassment.) See "A Brief History of Student-to-Student Sexual Harassment" in appendix C.
- State civil laws, such as those prohibiting sex discrimination in schools, may apply. Some states have "little Title IX" laws much like the federal Title IX law whose antidiscrimination provisions would similarly prohibit student-to-student sexual harassment. Some states have enacted anti-bullying statutes that might also prohibit student-to-student sexual harassment. Other state civil laws may also prohibit student-to-student sexual harassment.

- State criminal sexual assault and abuse laws prohibit many of the physical forms of sexual harassment.

  A ten-year-old Baltimore, MD, boy was criminally charged with committing a fourth-degree sexual offense and four counts of assault after allegedly snapping bra straps of fellow students and touching one girl's buttocks. The incidents involved five girls, ages 8–10. The boy was also suspended for three days.[7]

- State laws typically require that sexual abuse in schools be reported. Some educators are not aware that behavior that is illegal when perpetrated by adults upon children (such as sexual abuse and assault) is *also illegal* when it occurs with students as perpetrators of offenses upon other students. Just as these behaviors must be reported to authorities when an adult sexually abuses a child, they must also be reported when a student *engages in the same behavior toward another student*.
- State antistalking laws may apply, for example, where a student stalks another or when computers are used to threaten students.
- Protections stated in the U.S. Constitution may apply in some instances to harassment based on sex and sexual orientation.
- Additional federal, state, or local laws may also apply when other forms of discrimination (such as those based on disability, race, color, national origin, and sexual orientation) are combined with sexual harassment.
- Federal, state, or local laws prohibiting "hate crimes" may also apply.
- State and local laws may prohibit such behaviors as "indecent exposure" and "lewdness."
- Tort laws such as those covering "negligence" and "intentional infliction of emotional harm" have been used in peer harassment cases.
- State or local laws may prohibit discrimination on the basis of sexual orientation.
- State Board of Education rules and regulations that cover reporting of sexual abuse and assault and those that prohibit sexual harassment, including harassment on the basis of sexual orientation, may also apply.

Stopping sexual harassment when it occurs can often prevent a lawsuit against a school district. Districts are usually sued not because one student has sexually harassed another but because a school allowed the sexually harassing behavior to continue and ignored the fact that the children were being hurt and needed help.

Free Speech and Sexual Harassment

Sometimes students and staff erroneously believe that everyone has a right to free speech so that even sexually harassing conduct can be justified by and upheld by the Constitution.

Although freedom of speech as guaranteed by the Constitution applies to both written and oral speech, the right to free speech is not an absolute one—especially when a school is disrupted, a student's rights have been violated, or a threat has been made. For example, the U.S. Supreme Court has ruled that student conduct that disrupts class work is not protected by the Constitutional right to free speech. "[C]onduct by the student, in class or out of it, which for any reason—whether it stems from time, place or type of behavior—materially disrupts class work or involves substantial disorder or invasion of the rights of others is, of course, not immunized by the constitutional guarantee of freedom of speech."[8]

In another case, involving sexual innuendos in a student's speech to a school assembly, the Supreme Court stated that "the constitutional rights of students in public school are not automatically coextensive with the rights of adults in other settings."[9]

Additionally, the Supreme Court has upheld a principal's decision to remove two articles from a student newspaper when the "free speech" involved has the school's imprimatur.[10]

Freedom of speech generally applies to e-mail and the Internet in the same way as it applies to other forms of speech. Thus students' use of school computers to post sexually offensive or harassing materials can be prohibited by schools just as a school may prohibit lewd or vulgar speech on school grounds. A key issue in incidents occurring on and off school grounds is whether these incidents caused substantial disruption.[11]

Sexual Harassment Can Cost Schools Money

Schools are ultimately responsible for protecting children and culpable when they do not protect them.[12]

Katy Lyle's brother first told her about the sexual graffiti about her in the boy's bathroom of their high school. Her mother complained more than a dozen times to the school, requesting that it be removed. Despite promises to remove it, the graffiti remained for sixteen months (including two summers and Katy's entire junior year), increasing in vulgarity, including pornographic references to dogs and accusations that Katy was having sexual relations with her brother. As the graffiti increased, classmates put obscene drawings on her desk; others sent notes demanding sex with her; still others ridiculed her, such as the boy who yelled aloud at the school's crowded entrance hall, "Hey Katy, I took a [expletive] in your stall this morning." Even after the graffiti was finally removed, Katy still shut herself into her room to cry. Her parents brought one of the first student-to-student sexual harassment cases in the United States, filing charges with the Minnesota Department of Human Rights in 1989. The case was settled for $15,000.[13]

Tawnya Brawdy faced a gauntlet of boys for years who would gather around her and "moo" at her, calling her a cow. The taunting continued before school, during classes, during lunch throughout her high school years. When she asked the school for help, her teacher told her she would just have to put up with it. When the U.S. Department of Education investigated the complaint, they described it in a 211-page report. Brawdy sued her school district and received $20,000 in an out-of-court settlement.[14]

A few weeks after he started middle school, an eighth-grade boy held John (last name withheld) down with the help of another boy and tried to sexually assault him. He managed to get away. When he filed charges against his attacker (who was later sent to Juvenile Hall) some boys and girls harassed him for filing charges. Some children hit him at lunch and between classes. Some spat on him, and he was taunted on the school bus. Students called him "condom seller" and other vulgar names. Sometimes, boys would slam into him, and once while waiting for the school bus, a group of boys hit and kicked him. An acting principal told him to avoid kids who bothered him and said that calling them to the office might make things worse.

When the school did not respond to his mother's complaints, she filed a lawsuit. Orland Joint Union School District (California) settled the case for $55,000. This was one of the first settlements paid to a boy in a school sexual harassment case.[15]

In Petaluma, a middle school girl was called "slut" and "hot dog bitch" and other names by her classmates who also threatened to beat her and on one occasion slapped her face. Despite her repeated complaints to the school and some disciplinary action, the harassment continued. School officials were alleged to have said that "boys will be boys" and that eventually the harassers would mature and the harassment would stop. The case was settled for $250,000.[16]

The sixth grader in a California elementary school in Antioch was subjected to obscene gestures, demeaning comments about her body, and a near-daily barrage of vulgar verbal insults and violent threats by one of her male classmates. When the school did not respond to the parents' complaints, they went to court. A jury awarded the girl and her family $500,000. The child's father said the lawsuit had cost him most of the family's savings, about $150,000.[17]

Beginning in seventh grade, James Nabozny was verbally harassed by other students because of his sexual orientation. In one of two incidents when he was assaulted in school bathrooms, he fell into a urinal and one of the students then urinated on him. He was also kicked in the stomach in a school hallway, causing internal bleeding. Twice during his high school years he attempted suicide.

Although he repeatedly reported the harassment and assaults, the school did not fulfill its promise to act on the complaints. The principal was also alleged to have said "boys will be boys" and that if he was going to be so openly gay he should expect such treatment from his classmates. Another school official stated Nabozny "deserved such treatment because he is gay."

After a jury found that school officials had violated Nabozny's constitutional rights through intentional discrimination, a settlement was reached for $900,000 plus up to an additional $62,000 for medical expenses.[18]

WHY DOES SEXUAL HARASSMENT HAPPEN?

Any Student Can Become a Harasser

Students may be exploring their sexuality, and some may be unsure how to behave. They may be imitating behaviors they have seen at home, on computers or television, in movies or videos.

By the age of nineteen our children have spent nearly 19,000 hours in front of television (compared with only 16,000 hours in school), and nearly two-thirds of all television programming has sexual content. Between 1998 and 1999, the number of sexual references on television more than tripled.[19]

On many sitcoms, sexual harassment is not only commonplace, but typically presented in a manner that makes it seem acceptable. In one study, 36 percent of the sexually harassing behavior was welcomed by the target of the behavior; in 24 percent of the incidents there was no visible reaction, and in 40 percent the targets did not welcome the behavior. The behaviors seem acceptable because they are accompanied by laugh tracks and there are no consequences for the person who initiated the harassing behavior. In none of the incidents was anyone sanctioned or told that a behavior was out of line.[20]

Some students are deliberately trying to intimidate or humiliate another student. They may need to feel "powerful," and sexually harassing someone makes them feel stronger, bigger, and better than their victims. Others are imitating their peers who are harassing or may go along with their friends who harass because they are frightened of losing their friendship. Some students believe that sexually harassing behavior is the way sexuality is "normally" expressed or is a way to confirm their own sexuality. However, sexual harassment is less about sexuality than an assertion of dominance.

Some students harass weaker students because they have learned to relate to others primarily by intimidation. Others use sexual harassment to get attention from other students.

Students who engage in harassing behaviors typically learn that sexual bullying pays off. They begin to believe that relationships between men and women are based on the power to hurt another person. They are learning destructive ways of relating to their peers, exhibiting behaviors that are not only illegal but also harmful to themselves and others. All of these behaviors limit the harasser's ability to develop lifelong positive social skills and can have a serious impact on their future behavior at college, at work, and in personal relationships.

- "If I stand up to a male jerk at school, he automatically calls me a bitch."[21]

- When schools tolerate student-to-student harassment, the behavior often spills over to [their] teachers, especially female teachers who many be shoved, pelted with wads of papers, and called "bitch," "whore," and other names. Students grow up believing that these behaviors are acceptable and may carry the same behavior to college.[22]
- The four young men, all first-year students at a prestigious undergraduate college, were working in pairs. One would block a woman student, and then the other would grab her crotch from behind. Several of the women complained to the dean of students, who met with each of the men individually to discuss their behavior. Although all had gone to different high schools, their reaction was identical—"But everybody did this in high school!" They had no understanding that their behavior was unacceptable or that in most, if not all, states it would constitute a criminal offense of sexual abuse or assault.[23]
- A study of nearly 2,000 high school girls by the Harvard School of Public Health found that one in five reported being the victim of physical or sexual violence. Girls reported being "hit, shoved or forced into sexual activity" by dates.[24]

SEXUAL HARASSMENT AFFECTS ALL STUDENTS

Any Student Can Become a Victim

Girls are more likely to be harassed than boys. Girls are typically harassed because of their appearance. "Unattractive" or "unstylish" girls as well as girls who are physically mature are at higher risk. Girls of color may be at higher risk than other girls. *Boys are often harassed by boys as well as by girls.* Typically, boys are harassed because of how they behave. Boys who do not fit the stereotypic male image are more likely to be harassed and called names such as "fag," "queer," "sissy." Those who do not excel in athletics are often targets. Male-to-male sexual harassment is often not seen as sexual harassment, or if noticed, the sexual aspects are ignored and the behavior is more likely to be called bullying.[25]

Students for whom English is a second language and *students who are small or very shy* as well as *students who are being bullied* are also more likely to be sexually harassed.

Disabled girls are also at risk. Disabled students are often unable to protect themselves either verbally or physically. Thus, they are more vulnerable to sexually harassing behaviors.

Students who are harassed may exhibit:

- Fear of coming to school—they may avoid classes or certain areas of school
- Fear of the person(s) harassing them
- Inability to concentrate or learn
- Angry feelings and behavior
- Confused feelings
- Physical symptoms such as insomnia, headaches, stomachaches, and loss of appetite
- Feelings of being isolated from other children and subsequent withdrawal from social interactions
- Blaming oneself for the harassment
- Feelings of shame about sexuality
- Feelings of humiliation
- Feelings of worthlessness, vulnerability, and anxiety
- Depression—some children have contemplated or attempted suicide.

Students who fail to get support from school and/or parents are at even greater risk for depression, isolation from peers and family, and suicidal thoughts.

Sometimes alcohol, drug abuse, and smoking can be a reaction to sexual harassment.

Adults who have been bullied remember feeling angry, upset, frustrated, and fearful. Students who are sexually harassed have the same feelings. The impact of being sexually harassed is long-lasting and often leaves permanent scars; victims of sexual harassment often need counseling and guidance. The motivation to learn can be damaged when a student has to constantly deal with sexual harassment at school. Fear can make a student feel that he or she does not "belong."

Someone said that I was a slut. You always try to pretend that what people say about you doesn't affect you, but it does. You slowly start to believe what's being said about you. (teenage girl)[26]

Girls are more likely to gain a reputation of "slut" and being sexually available than boys. "A reputation acquired in young adolescence can damage a woman's self-esteem for years no matter how smart or talented she is. She may become a target for other forms of sexual harassment. She may be raped. She may become promiscuous, figuring she might as well do what she is accused of doing. Or she may shut down her sexual side entirely, wearing baggy clothes and sticking close to home."[27]

> I really think sexual harassment can hurt because sometimes people may tease you about your body parts and it really hurts your feelings because you can't change them in any way. It can also interfere with your schoolwork because all your thoughts are on your anger and then you can't concentrate. If I am harassed in the future, I will stand up for my rights and if a teacher doesn't care, I will pressure him or her to punish my harasser.[28]

Students who are not harassed but see it happening to others also feel vulnerable and fear that they will be the next victim.[29] Some may even be wary of showing sympathy to those who are harassed. Acceptance of peer sexual harassment by victims and bystanders can set the stage for future sexual abuse and assault by "teaching" students that sexual hostility is "normal" and acceptable.

WHY STUDENTS DON'T REPORT SEXUAL HARASSMENT

- I felt like the teacher (who was a man) betrayed me and thought I was making a big deal out of nothing. But most of all, I felt . . . it made me feel slutty and cheap. It made me feel . . . we shouldn't have to put up with that stuff, but no one will do anything to stop it. Now sexual harassment doesn't bother me as much because it happens so much it almost seems normal. . . . The longer it goes on without anyone doing anything, the more I think of it as one of those things that I have to put up with.[30]
- No way I'd report harassment to the principal or anyone else. I'd be the laughingstock of the school. (girl from Long Island, N.Y.)[31]

Many students who experience sexual harassment suffer in silence and do not report it. Studies vary in the percentage of students who report sexual harassment to adults. One study reported that only 6 percent told an adult. The rest told a friend or told no one.[32] The landmark AAUW study *Hostile Hallways 2001* reported that only 11 percent of the students who experience nonphysical harassment told a teacher, 9 percent told another employee, and 20 percent told no one, including friends or parents. For physical harassment, the figures were similar: 11 percent told a teacher, 9 percent told another employee, and 20 percent told no one.[33]

The reasons are many:

- They may not be sure or know that the behavior is sexual harassment or prohibited.
- They may be afraid that no one will believe them.
- They don't think anyone will do anything to stop it or that nothing will happen.
- They don't believe adults will help them.
- They may have told an adult previously and not received help.
- They don't know how the school will handle it.
- They worry that they will be blamed for the harassment, or they think it's their fault that the harassment occurred, that is, they "deserve" it.
- They are frightened that if they complain, the harassment might get worse.
- They worry that there may be retaliation from the person harassing them and that person's friends.
- They worry that their friends may taunt and ridicule them for bringing a complaint.
- They think that they ought to be able to handle it alone.

In many schools there is a "code of silence" and students worry they will be penalized for "tattling" or "snitching" (see "Breaking the Code of Silence" in chapter 5).

When students do report harassment and ask for help it is often because the harassment has increased in frequency and severity and/or the student has been unable to stop it and can no longer tolerate it.

Some schools have hotlines where students can call for help with a variety of problems; others have hotlines to report students' threats of violence or possession of weapons. These could be expanded to deal with sexual harassment issues.

WHERE DOES SEXUAL HARASSMENT FREQUENTLY OCCUR?

Sexual harassment occurs in all kinds of schools—public, private, urban, suburban, rural, large, and small. It happens in classrooms, stairways, hallways, cafeterias, school buses, locker areas, on the playground, and on the way to and from school. It often occurs in the presence of adults. In schools where sexual harassment is tolerated and ignored, students are more likely to engage in these kinds of behavior.

School buses are common places for harassment and even assault.

- On a bus for a suburban Virginia middle school a thirteen-year-old boy held a thirteen-year-old girl down while another thirteen-year-old boy fondled her. In the same school in the previous three months, there were four incidents of boys touching girls on the breast or buttocks.[34]
- "One of my sixth-graders came to me the other day and said a boy was undoing her pants on the bus."[35]
- The behavior had gone unreported until a substitute bus driver reported that two of the boys were grinding their hips together.[36]
- A boy on the school bus drew pictures of naked girls and added genitalia to a picture drawn by a girl. Boys on the bus were making sexual comments.[37]
- A suit against a Massachusetts school district charged that the district did not respond adequately to parents' complaint that their five-year-old kindergarten daughter was often persuaded by a nine-year-old boy to raise her dress and pull down her underwear while traveling on the school bus. The girl added that the boy would then force her to spread her legs apart while other children watched and laughed. In addition to asking for $3.75 million the parents have also asked to order the district to place adult monitors on all school buses and to establish a policy on peer harassment.[38]

Bathrooms can be dangerous too. In one month during 1997, the following incidents were publicized:

- A fourteen-year-old Colorado high school student reported that a group of boys dragged her into a bathroom and tried to remove her pants.
- A girl was raped by a boy in a Florida middle school girls' bathroom while a second boy held her down.
- A thirteen-year-old New York student reported that she was twice forced to perform oral sex in the boys' bathroom.[39]

Bad things happen in cafeterias, playgrounds, gyms, locker rooms, stairways, and elsewhere:

- A group of boys stood around a sophomore girl in the cafeteria and forced her to bend over, hands between her legs, as they taunted her. (From a diary kept by a high school senior, recording incidents of sexual behaviors)[40]
- Four third-grade boys in Maine sexually assaulted their nine-year-old classmate by pinning her to the ground while one boy lay on top of her and simulated sex. When she complained to the playground supervisor, she was told to "stay away from the boys," and another attack occurred two days later.[41]
- The boy put a doorstop in his pants, pretended it was his penis, and chased several girls around the gym, making sexual comments as he did so.[42]
- Today in class people reported their finding as ethnographers; that is, they told the class about the examples of sexual harassment they had witnessed. There were some pretty bad examples. It's amazing that this stuff goes on in our school. I think that part of the problem is that some kids don't know what sexual harassment is, so they don't know when they are doing it. Everybody found at least one or two examples, and most people found many more. I found out that it happens everywhere; in the halls, in the cafeteria, or even at basketball try-outs. It happens everywhere that teachers are not in direct supervision of students. (eighth-grade male student)[43]

- First girl: "I hate it when on the stairway a guy from behind grabs your genitals." Second girl: "Yeah, you never know who it is because the stairs are so crowded." Third girl: "It's awful." (Comments from three Montgomery County, Maryland, high school girls during a televised interview about a sexual assault at their school.)
- His teammates on his high school football team taped his genitals, tied him to a towel rack in the locker room, and then called in classmates to see him. When he complained, he was suspended and then kicked off the team. The rest of the football season was cancelled, but his teammates were never disciplined.[44]

TEN MYTHS ABOUT STUDENT-TO-STUDENT SEXUAL HARASSMENT

1. *"Sexual harassment is just part of normal development. It's part of growing up."*

    While it is true that often youngsters test out behaviors, they need to learn which of these behaviors are unacceptable. When students are allowed to engage in hurtful behaviors they are not learning the skills they need for life.

2. *"Normal boy–girl relationships are not allowed anymore. All this stuff about sexual harassment gets in the way of boys and girls learning to relate to each other in a friendly manner."*

    Unwanted sexual innuendos, lewd comments, grabbing, and touching are not expressions of friendship nor are they the type of social relationships that students should be having with each other. Flirting and sexual harassment are very different behaviors. In flirting, the behavior is welcomed and is characterized by the respect each has for the other. Either person can stop the flirting, unlike sexual harassment. Flirting makes people feel good; harassment makes them feel bad. Often the purpose of sexual harassment is deliberate humiliation or embarrassment.

3. *"Girls get sexually harassed because they are asking for it. If they wouldn't dress provocatively we would not have a problem with sexual harassment."*

Sexual harassment can happen to anyone, no matter how they dress. The way students dress does not give someone else permission to touch them, make lewd comments, or otherwise harass them. Sexual harassment has much more to do with power and the use of sexuality to intimidate than with sexual attractiveness or appearance. Focusing on girls' clothing puts the responsibility on girls rather than on the student doing the harassing.

4. *"Sexual harassment only happens to girls."*

Although girls are more likely to be harassed, boys too can be harassed both by girls and other boys. Girls are sometimes harassed by other girls.

5. *"If students would just say 'No' or just ignore sexual harassment, it would stop."*

Saying "No" or "I want you to stop that" doesn't work all the time. Many boys believe that girls really like their behavior and believe that girls don't really mean it when they say "No." Thus a girl's "no" often becomes justification for continuing the sexual harassment. In most instances, ignoring harassment does not stop it. Indeed, the harassment may actually get worse. Not responding is often viewed as either "she likes what I said" or "she is too weak to stop me."

6. *"Sexual harassment is no big deal. People who complain usually don't have a sense of humor or don't know how to accept a compliment."*

Sexually intimidating behavior is not a compliment nor is it funny. Harassment is often painful and frightening. No one should have to accept sexual humiliation with a smile. Harassing comments about one's sexuality make many students very uncomfortable.

7. *"Sexual harassment is often unintentional."*

Whether the person meant to harass someone else is not relevant. The behavior is just as hurtful whether it is intentional or not.

8. *"Learning how to handle these behaviors will make students stronger."*

Sexual harassment does not make people stronger; in fact, it makes students feel weak, powerless, and sometimes angry. It can have life-long negative impact. We do not tolerate sexual harassment in adults or expect them to be able to deal with it on their own. Should we expect children to do so or to tolerate behaviors we do not tolerate in adults?

9. *"It's just the way boys show they like girls."*

The assumption that hurtful behavior is an *acceptable* way of showing affection sets up males and females for future abusive relationships. *No one should have to endure hurtful behavior.*

10. *"The law has gone too far. Boys and girls can get in trouble for almost anything."*

The Supreme Court, in a Title IX case, was very careful in applying the term *sexual harassment* to student misconduct. The behavior has to be so severe, pervasive, and objectively offensive that it effectively deprives the harassed student of access to educational opportunities. However, even if the behavior does not breach the law, sexually harassing behavior should not be tolerated in any school.[45]

NOTES

1. "Says She Was Sexually Harassed in 6th Grade," *New York Times*, November 4, 1996.

2. N. Stein, "Sexual Harassment in K–12 Schools: The Public Performance of Gendered Violence," *Harvard Educational Review* 65, 2 (Summer 1995).

3. J. Adler and D. Rosenburg, "Must Boys Always Be Boys?" *Newsweek*, October 19, 1992, p. 77.

4. Related to authors.

5. *Harassment-Free Hallways: How to Stop Sexual Harassment in Schools* (Washington, D.C.: American Association of University Women, Educational Foundation, 2002; updated in 2004), II-3.1

6. A. Van Buren, Dear Abby Letter from "Three Girls from Zanesville, Ohio," *Washington Post*, January 18 2003, p. C-10.

7. "10-Year Old Charged after Snapping Bras, Touching Girl," *The Baltimore Sun*, May 28, 1999, as described in *Educator's Guide to Controlling Sexual Harassment*, Monthly Bulletin, July 1999, p. 8.

8. *Tinker v. Des Moines Independent Community School District*, 393 U.S. 503 (1969).

9. *Fraser v. Bethel School District No. 403*, 478 U.S. 675, 682 (1986).

10. *Hazelwood School District v. Kuhlmeier*, 484 U.S. 260 (1988).

11. S. Permuth, *A Legal Memorandum: The Internet, Students' Rights and Today's Principal.* (Reston, Va.: National Association of Secondary School Principals, 1998).

12. L. Walls, *Bullying and Sexual Harassment in Schools.* n.d. Retrieved June 26, 2004 from www.cfchildren.org/article_walls1.html (Committee for Children).

13. C. Gorny, "Teaching Johnny the Appropriate Way to Flirt." *New York Times Magazine*, June 13, 1999, pp. 43–47, 67, 73, 80, 82, 83.

14. Adler and Rosenberg.

15. K. Seligman, "Boys Join List of the Sexually Harassed," *San Francisco Examiner*, November 17, 1996, pp. A-1, A-16.

16. "$250,000 Settlement Reached in Petaluma Peer Harassment Case," *Educator's Guide to Controlling Sexual Harassment,* Monthly Bulletin, October 1997, p. 1, 3.

17. S. Holt and M. Weiser, "Antioch Schools Lose Sex Lawsuit," *Contra Costa Times*, October 2, 1996; S. E. Solis, "Price of Victory in Harass Suit," *San Francisco Chronicle*, October 3, 1996, pp. A17, A20.

18. "School District Reaches Settlement with Former Student for Over $900,000," *Educator's Guide to Controlling Sexual Harassment,* Monthly Bulletin, February 1997, pp. 1–2.

19. D. Roffman, "Dangerous Games: A Sex Video Broke the Rules. But for Kids the Rules Have Changed," *Washington Post*, April 15, 2001, pp. B1, B4. Data quoted from Parents Television Council.

20. B. Sandler, "Why Sexual Harassment Continues: Reinforcement on Television," *About Women on Campus*, National Association for Women in Education (Summer 1995), pp. 7–8.

21. P. Haag, *Voices of a Generation, Teenage Girls on Sex, School, and Self* (Washington, D.C.: American Association of University Women, Educational Foundation, 1999), p. 21.

22. J. Carroll, "Dealing with Nasty Students," *The Chronicle of Higher Education*, May 2, 2003, p. C5.

23. Related to one of the authors.

24. A. Dickinson, "When Dating Is Dangerous," *Time*, August 27, 2001.

25. C. Shakeshaft, L. Mandel, Y. M. Johnson, J. Sawyer, M. A. Hergenrother, and E. Barber, "Boys Call Me Cow," *Educational Leadership* 5, 2 (1997): 23–24.

26. Haag, *Voices of a Generation*, p. 23.

27. L. Stepp, "When 'Good Girls' Get a Bad Rep," *Washington Post*, August 24, 1999, p. C4

28. Stein, "Sexual Harassment in K–12 Schools."

29. *Hostile Hallways & Bullying: Teasing and Sexual Harassment in School* (Washington, D.C.: American Association of University Women Educational Foundation, 2001), p. 36.

30. N. Stein, "No Laughing Matter: Sexual Harassment in K–12 Schools," in *Transforming a Rape Culture*, ed. E. Buckwald (Minneapolis: Milleweed Editions, 1993), pp. 331–14.

31. Shakeshaft et al., "Boys Call Me Cow."

32. Shakeshaft et al., "Boys Call Me Cow."

33. *Hostile Hallways*, p. 29, figures 20 and 21.

34. J. Comiteau, "2 Charged in School Bus Sex Assault," *Fairfax VA Journal*, June 11, 1992.

35. "Sex Harassment Increasing Amid Students, Officials Say," *Boston Globe*, February 4, 1999.

36. "Boy Charged with Groping and Assaulting Girls on Bus," *Educator's Guide to Controlling Sexual Harassment,* Monthly Bulletin, July 2002, p. 10.

37. "Missouri School District Wins Dismissal of Peer Harassment Suit," *Educator's Guide to Controlling Sexual Harassment,* Monthly Bulletin, June 1998, p. 7.

38. "Parents Sue School District after Child Harassed on Bus," *Educator's Guide to Controlling Sexual Harassment,* Monthly Bulletin, May 2002, p. 9.

39. "Spate of Sexual Assaults in Bathrooms Raises Liability Questions," *Educator's Guide to Controlling Sexual Harassment,* Monthly Bulletin, December 1997, pp. 1–3.

40. "Sex Harassment Increasing Amid Students, Officials Say."

41. "Outrage of the School Year," *Washington Feminist Faxnet*, Center for the Advancement of Public Policy, June 16, 2000, p. 1.

42. *Davis v. Monroe County Board of Education*, 119 S. Ct. 1661 (1999).

43. Stein, "Sexual Harassment in K-12 Schools."

44. K. Seligman, "Boys Join List of the Sexually Harassed," *San Francisco Examiner*, November 17, 1996. Retrieved June 26, 2004, from www.sfgate.com.

45. *Davis v. Monroe County Board of Education*, 119 S. Ct. 1661 (1999).

CHAPTER 3

How to Build a Comprehensive Program

Student-to-student harassment has educational, social, psychological, and legal implications. More than simple goodwill is needed to prevent and deal with it. This chapter describes actions that a district should undertake, including the development of an effective wide-ranging policy.

This chapter can be used to identify the elements necessary to develop effective policies and programs and includes the following topics:

Responsibilities of the School Superintendent
How to Assess the Extent of Peer Harassment in the District and School
    Environments
Worried about Publicizing the District's "Dirty Laundry?"
How to Evaluate Your Current Policy or Develop a New One

RESPONSIBILITIES OF THE SCHOOL SUPERINTENDENT

Depending on the district's organization, the responsibilities of the school superintendent may be carried out by the principal, vice principal, sexual harassment administrator, or site complaint manager. When the word *administrator* appears in this book, those responsibilities listed may also be performed by any of these persons.

The superintendent sets the stage for a successful policy and program to prevent and deal with sexual harassment, and is responsible for the following critical actions:

- Appoint one person to be in charge of sexual harassment issues for the district. This designated person, often referred to as the sexual harassment administrator, is the superintendent's representative who can guide the process and many of the activities listed in this section. Title IX requires that each educational entity (the district) designate a "responsible employee" whose responsibility is to co-ordinate the efforts to comply with Title IX, including sexual ha-rassment, and to handle sexual discrimination complaints. The per-son designated to handle sexual harassment, in some instances, is the Title IX coordinator; in other instances, that person works with the Title IX coordinator.

- Provide a written job description for the sexual harassment ad-ministrator that includes responsibility for:
  - —developing and implementing programs
  - —training of all staff
  - —coordination with school personnel and programs
  - —coordination with the district's attorney
  - —development of materials
  - —dissemination
  - —training activities
  - —handling complaints
  - —record keeping
  - —developing family and community relationships
  - —monitoring the policy
  - —appointment and supervision of site complaint managers
  - —periodic reporting to the superintendent and the community
  - —preparation of an annual report on sexual harassment for the su-perintendent and the board of education.
- Ensure that the sexual harassment administrator for the district re-ceives appropriate training periodically, has sufficient resources (time, availability of staff, etc.), and is evaluated annually. Simi-larly, ensure that the persons responsible for receiving complaints at the building or site level receive specific training and meet reg-ularly to exchange information and identify problems.
- Meet on a regular basis with this person in order to stay informed and to provide guidance where necessary.
- Appoint a committee to work with the sexual harassment adminis-trator. The committee should include administrators, principals, teachers, nonprofessional staff, guidance personnel, students, and

community members. It should include people of color, men, and women.

- Publicize the appointment of that person and the committee so that everyone is informed.
- Charge the committee with the development of an action plan, including a school-based intervention plan and a timetable for implementation. Include a date by which the plan will be completed.
- Be knowledgeable about the existing district sexual harassment policy and any other policies that are related to it, such as those that deal with discipline and bullying. Meet with the district's attorney and ensure that he or she is familiar with student sexual harassment issues and keeps up to date with new developments.
- Involve all members of the school community to prevent and respond to student harassment.
- Ensure that there is an assessment of the district and school environments to evaluate the extent of student-to-student harassment. Often administrators, staff, students, and families may believe that sexual harassment only happens in *other* schools, not theirs. Assessment becomes important because it plays an immediate and important role in educating the district, its employees, students, and the community about the existence and importance of student-to-student sexual harassment and in establishing the direction the district needs to go. ("How to Assess the Extent of Peer Harassment in the District and School Environments" appears on page 36.)
- Ensure that there is a comprehensive sexual harassment policy. (See "How to Evaluate Your Current Policy or Develop a New One," page 39, which describes the development and elements of an effective policy.)
- Ensure that sexual harassment is included in the district's and schools' discipline policies.
- Monitor training programs for all persons in the school system:
  —administrators
  —teachers
  —staff, including: aides and assistants, bus drivers, cafeteria workers, grounds persons, crossing guards, coaches, and police liaison and security officers
  —volunteers

—students
—families

All new employees and incoming and transfer students should receive training and information as part of their introduction to the district and their school. If the sexual harassment administrator is not responsible for ongoing training (as in the case when there is a separate training division), ensure that a specific individual is directly responsible for ongoing sexual harassment training.

- Ensure that adequate resources and time are allocated for training. Training is discussed in greater detail in chapter 4.
- Ensure that there is an information and dissemination program to educate and periodically remind personnel, students, and families about sexual harassment. Chapter 5 describes how to disseminate the sexual harassment policy and how to help students learn about harassment.
- Support the development of a district or school-wide code of behavior and/or Student Bill of Rights that encourages respect among students, including consequences for breaking the rules.
- Ensure that there is a process to inform all personnel in writing to take all complaints from students, families, teachers, and staff seriously.
- Ensure that staff at all levels understand that they have an obligation to report to an appropriate person any sexual harassment that they observe or learn about.
- Ensure that guidelines, such as the following, are used to evaluate whether complaints are being handled effectively:
  —Ensure that the behavior stops.
  —Investigate the behavior if necessary. (Do not excuse behaviors by describing them as "boys will be boys" or as the result of "cultural differences.")
  —Apply sanctions.
  —Keep written records of all that happens.
  —Notify families.
  —Implement other steps necessary for preventing a recurrence of the behavior.

A high school sophomore was the only girl on the boy's ice hockey team (there was no team for girls). Her teammates and other classmates called her "stupid bitch," "dyke," "a he-she," "a man-wannabe," and other names. Sexual rumors were spread about her. She was pushed against her locker. When she was on crutches following surgery, someone pulled the crutches away from her.

Her mother called the athletic director five times, leaving messages as to why she was calling, and none of the calls were returned. Similar calls to the assistant coach, head coach, dean of students, and principal were not returned. The parents pulled the child out of school and contacted a lawyer.[1]

- Ensure that a process is instituted to regularly monitor how well the policy is working within the district and at the school level. This can be the responsibility of school committees working within the district.
- Require an annual report on sexual harassment. ("What to Include in Annual Reports" appears in appendix A.)
- Require that the district and schools maintain data including:
  - summary of cases reported
  - number of cases handled formally and informally
  - description of each case and how it was resolved

  This information should be transmitted regularly to the superintendent and the school board. (A checklist appears in appendix A.)

- Conduct periodic meetings of district and school administrators, including principals, to ensure that they are aware of their obligation to prevent, intervene, and stop sexual harassment. The sexual harassment administrator should be at these meetings not only to provide help and information, but also to learn about the problems faced by administrators. If the district has its own attorney, it is helpful for that person to attend these meetings.
- Ensure that there is a policy to examine all buildings and outdoor areas for graffiti at least once annually, and develop ways to remove it or paint it over. Ensure that graffiti that is reported at other times is removed or covered over quickly.
- Ensure that there is adequate supervision of cafeterias, playgrounds, stairways and halls, and buses—common places for peer harassment to occur. If teachers are not available, use aides and volunteers.

- Ensure that all employees carrying out their responsibilities concerning sexual harassment are indemnified against unreasonable lawsuits by students or their families.

Sample Agenda for a Meeting of Administrators on Student-to-Student Sexual Harassment

- Definition of sexual harassment with examples
- Summary of key elements of policy
- Legal implications
- Staff obligations in dealing with sexual harassment
- How to intervene when observing sexual harassment
- What needs to be improved:
  — what do personnel need to know
  — assessment of prevention activities currently in place
- Next steps

(See chapter 4 for a detailed outline.)

HOW TO ASSESS THE EXTENT OF PEER HARASSMENT IN THE DISTRICT AND SCHOOL ENVIRONMENTS

Assessment is important because it plays an immediate and important role in educating staff, students, and the community about the importance of student-to-student sexual harassment and establishes the direction that the district and schools need to go.

Assessment is often thought of in terms of formal surveys and questionnaires. While these techniques are indeed useful, they are time-consuming and expensive to develop, administer, and interpret.

Other means of assessment include the following:

- Ask personnel to submit examples and any concerns or questions they have about student-to-student sexual harassment. Questions such as the following could be sent out in advance:
  — How extensive do you think student-to-student harassment is?
  — Have you observed it? If so, what kinds of incidents?

—When did you see it happen?
—Are you comfortable intervening in an incident?
—Are you familiar with the district policy?
—Are you familiar with your responsibilities and obligations?
—What do you need to know about sexual harassment?
—What actions would you like to see the school (or district) take?

Information could be submitted informally or brought to a meeting.

- Collect information informally. Teachers and administrators can ask school personnel, students, and families if they have observed peer harassment. (Teachers should be asked to name students whom they have observed harassing others or being harassed. The names of these students should be disseminated *privately* to appropriate staff on a need-to-know basis, with a *plan to respond and prevent further harassment.*)
- Meet with a group or groups of students, staff, or volunteers and ask if they have observed student-to-student sexual harassment, the extent of the problem, what actions the school needs to take, etc. ("How to Conduct a Student Discussion about Sexual Harassment," including guidelines, appears in chapter 7.
- Routinely ask students who drop vocational or academic classes, request transfers, or drop out of school what their reasons are and explore whether sexual harassment was a factor in their decision.
- Train students as observers. One inexpensive but effective way to assess the extent of sexual harassment is to train several students, males and females (at least fifth grade or higher), to record incidents they observe. In a two-hour meeting, the students are taught what behaviors are considered sexual harassment and how to record their observations. (Teachers and other staff can be similarly trained to observe and report incidents.)
    —The task of the observers is to write down every incident of student-to-student harassment they see within a one- or two-week period. The written description should not include names. However, they should be told to report, with names if

possible, serious incidents (such as touching) to the appropriate person. The student observers should also be instructed what to say if other students ask what they are doing, such as they "have an assignment from the counselor" or from whoever is doing the assessment. Observers should report all incidents even when they are not certain that the behavior is sexual harassment.

— The observers are given a notebook or several copies of a form with questions such as those listed in the "Sample Incident Report" which appears on page 39.

— At the end of the observation period, the notebooks or forms are likely to provide a sizeable number of incidents that can be used to educate the school community about the extent of sexual harassment.

— A summary of incidents, including some of the descriptions, can be presented orally or in written form to administrators, staff, students, and their families. The incidents can also be presented by students at an assembly and/or at a meeting of administrators, principals, families, and/or students. (Incidents should be reported in such a manner that no one is able to tell which students were involved.)

— Describing actual incidents helps everyone understand the prevalence of sexual harassment and helps develop support for the sexual harassment policy and its implementation. This activity also indicates the commitment of the district and individual schools to ending student-to-student sexual harassment.

WORRIED ABOUT PUBLICIZING THE DISTRICT'S "DIRTY LAUNDRY"?

Many districts worry that reporting incidents will result in bad publicity about sexual harassment in their schools. Yet without a strong awareness of the problem, individuals may be reluctant to deal with harassment issues. One way for the district to deal with potentially negative publicity is to point out publicly that peer sexual harassment is a *national* problem in schools, but in *this* district something is being done about the issue rather than ignoring it.

Sample Incident Report

Observer Incident Report

(Write on the back of this page or on another sheet of paper if you need
     more room for any of the questions.)

Date of the incident _____

Where did the incident occur _____

Who acted in a sexually harassing manner   # of boys _____
     # of girls _____

Who was the victim(s)?   # of boys _____   # of girls _____

What happened?

How did the victim respond to the harassment?

Approximate number of other students present (if any):
     boys _____   girls _____

Did any adults see what happened?   Yes _____   No _____

If yes, how many _____

Were any of the adults teachers?   Yes _____   No _____

How did the adults respond?

Anything else about the incident you would like to add:

Reported written by _____   Grade _____

Please submit this form to _____

Material to be covered in a sexual harassment reporting form appears
     in appendix A.

HOW TO EVALUATE YOUR CURRENT POLICY OR DEVELOP A NEW ONE

Title IX of the Education Amendments of 1972 prohibits sex discrimination, including student-to-student sexual harassment, in educational entities (such as districts) receiving any federal funds. Title IX also requires
schools to have a policy prohibiting sex discrimination, including grievance procedures for addressing complaints, and to appoint a person in
charge of Title IX grievance procedures, such as the Title IX coordinator.

Title IX does not require schools to have a separate sexual harassment policy, provided that the more general sex discrimination policy
also applies to sexual harassment. Nevertheless, almost all schools

find it beneficial to have a separate sexual harassment policy. *Even if a district does not have a written policy, the law still prohibits student-to-student sexual harassment.*

Most of the current sexual harassment policies were developed initially to deal with sexual harassment of employees and sexual harassment of students by teachers and other staff at a time when little attention was paid to peer sexual harassment. Thus many school policies cover student-to-student harassment only by inference or not at all; in many policies, peer harassment is not mentioned. When student-to-student harassment is not mentioned specifically in the policy nor given sufficient emphasis, readers may not fully understand the importance of this issue or even understand that it is prohibited by the policy and by federal and state laws.

It is important that districts evaluate their policy to specifically include peer harassment, and to assess whether the current policy needs to be changed so that student-to-student harassment is clearly and effectively defined. (Individual schools can supplement district policy with additional rules specific to their school.)

If the policy dealing with student-to-student harassment is part of the general sexual harassment policy, it should define student-to-student sexual harassment as clearly separate from that part of the policy covering adults who harass other adults or students. The consequences for student behaviors (in contrast to those for professional and nonprofessional staff) also need to be delineated separately.

The following section will be helpful to districts that are developing a student-to-student sexual harassment policy for the first time, and to those districts that want to evaluate their existing policy. It is divided into two parts: "The Policy Process" and "Elements of a Good Policy."

The Policy Process

How well the policy will be accepted by the educational community it will serve is directly related to the way in which a policy is adopted or revised. Policies that are developed outside the district and simply adopted by top administrators or revised without input from the educational community are unlikely to have widespread support. In contrast, policies that are adopted or revised with the involvement of many people are better understood and are more likely to be supported and implemented by wide segments of the community. The process itself, developing or revising an existing policy, can serve as a tool for educating members of the educational community.

Policies are written documents that need to be updated from time to time because of new legal developments, new knowledge about sexual harassment, and inadvertent omissions in the policy. In some instances the policy may not have worked as well as expected and may need some revisions or fine tuning.

Strategies listed below are helpful when a district is developing a new policy or evaluating its current policy:

- Develop or revise the policy with involvement of key administrators, teachers, staff, district's attorney, and members of the community. Appoint a committee representing all segments of the district to work on the policy development or evaluation and/or revision of existing policy. Policies developed by such a group are more likely to be understood, supported, and implemented.
- Ensure that one person is in charge of the policy process, usually the sexual harassment coordinator.
- Ensure that the persons involved in writing or revising the policy are knowledgeable about sexual harassment issues. The district's attorney and the sexual harassment coordinator should be involved. Discussion with students who have experienced sexual harassment and used the procedures, and staff who have responded to sexual harassment complaints, can help inform and educate the committee. Additionally, other sources of written information should be examined by the committee. Information for the prospective policy can also be obtained at open meetings from staff and families and at presentations at ongoing meetings.
- Examine other districts' policies, especially those of similar districts. However, no assumption should be made that other policies are automatically good models to follow.
- Examine state laws that prohibit discrimination on the basis of sex, race, and sexual orientation.
- Examine state criminal laws that prohibit sexual assault, sexual abuse, stalking, "indecent exposure," and "lewd behaviors."

- Examine State Board of Education rules, regulations, and guide-lines that prohibit discrimination based on sex, race, and sexual orientation, and cover sexual harassment. Additionally, examine teacher and school reporting requirements for sexual abuse and assault. [Note: Schools are generally required to report incidents to designated authorities such as child protection and law en-forcement officials.]
- Write the policy in simple language, not in legalese, such as de-scribing someone as "the party of the first part." The policy should be user friendly.
- Develop a deadline for the policy development or revision, so that it is completed within a reasonable time.
- Send draft copies to various members of the district and the community for comments before final adoption.
- Develop a process for periodic evaluation and revision of the policy.

Elements of a Good Policy[2]

The purpose of a sexual harassment policy is to:

- Demonstrate the district's and schools' commitment to prevent-ing and dealing with sexual harassment
- Educate employees, students, and families about the issues
- Set forth the procedures and sanctions for dealing with instances of sexual harassment
- Encourage staff and students to come forward with problems
- Comply with the requirements of Title IX and other federal and state laws where applicable.

The policy should include the following:

1. The name of the person in charge of sexual harassment issues, including title, location, phone, fax number, and e-mail address.
2. A short statement describing the district's commitment to pro-vide a positive learning and working environment. It should also state that the district does not tolerate sexual harassment in its

community. To this end, the district will provide the required periodic training for employees and students.

3. A definition of student-to-student harassment. Include examples to help readers understand the wide range of behaviors that are prohibited, such as sexual touching and name-calling, spreading rumors, graffiti, and computer harassment. Identify locations where incidents are most likely to occur. State that the sexual harassment prohibition covers males as well as females and includes same-sex harassment. Include a statement that intent is irrelevant in evaluating whether sexual harassment occurred. The policy should clearly state that sexually demeaning and harassing content on private and school websites and e-mails can be a violation of the policy not only when they are sent to one person but also when they are available to more than one person, such as on a website.

4. A description of who is covered by the policy (the entire school community, including all employees, students, visitors, volunteers, outside workers, contractors, and vendors).

5. A clearly stated prohibition against sexual harassment including a brief mention of relevant federal and state civil and criminal laws. Include a statement that the constitutional right to free speech cannot be used to justify or defend sexual harassment. (See "Is Sexual Harassment Illegal?" containing a list of laws that prohibit sexual harassment, in chapter 2.

6. A list of possible sanctions. A broad list of formal sanctions should be included, ranging from a written reprimand to expulsion.

7. Reporting and record-keeping requirements, including the reporting of *all* behaviors believed to be sexual harassment, whether or not the incident(s) is serious or handled informally. A person should be designated to be responsible for maintaining all records. Behaviors such as sexual abuse should also be reported to the school as well as to any required state or local authorities. Staff members observing student-to-student harassment or hearing about it should be required to report the behavior. Students and their families should also be encouraged to report to the teacher or other appropriate person any incidents that they observe or know about.

8. Persons to whom behavior can be reported should be listed by
   title, such as principal, vice principal, counselor, the sexual harassment administrator, and site complaint managers (as well as
   the person who is responsible for maintaining all records) and
   how they can be contacted. The actual names, along with title,
   office address, phone, e-mail, and fax, should be appended to the
   policy and periodically updated.

   At least one person in every building should be designated as
   the complaint manager for that site, including noneducational
   sites such as Physical Plant. (If possible, two persons, one male
   and one female, should be appointed.) The policy should make
   it clear, however, that individuals wishing to make a complaint
   can bypass their site complaint manager and take their complaint to any other complaint manager or administrator.
9. A statement that makes it clear that the confidentiality of the reporting student(s), witnesses, and bystanders will be observed,
   provided it does not interfere with the district's ability to investigate or take corrective action.
10. A statement that victims and witnesses will not be required to
    face their harassers. This should not preclude accused students
    from having an opportunity to explain their actions or refute the
    accusations. (When minors are involved, and in cases of sexual
    assault or abuse, it is well established that the victims should not
    be forced to face those who are accused of harming them.)
11. A description of the family notification process, including who
    is responsible for notification, who is notified, and a requirement
    that families of all the students involved be notified.
12. A strong prohibition of reprisals against anyone reporting sexual
    harassment behaviors, involved in handling a complaint, or par-
    ticipating in related activities. Include examples of retaliation,
    such as threats and encouraging others to retaliate. The policy
    should state that a finding of retaliation is independent of
    whether a charge or informal complaint is substantiated. The
    policy should also state that persons who report or complain
    about a sexual harassment incident they observed or know about
    are also protected from retaliation.
13. Ensure that the policy does not contradict state and federal
    nondiscrimination laws.

14. A statement that if charges are proven false, the district will take appropriate disciplinary action. Many people are concerned that students, particularly girls, will bring false charges against someone else. There is a little evidence to support this concern; to the contrary, it is difficult to get most students to report student-to-student sexual harassment in the first place. Although false charges are always a possibility, they are relatively rare.

15. A description of the formal complaint process. Although most complaints usually can be handled informally, a formal complaint process is critical for those incidents that cannot be handled in a less formal manner. The policy should also include a description of informal procedures or list where that information can be obtained (such as, in an appendix to the policy, a separate brochure, or from the person in charge of sexual harassment issues). Additionally, the policy should note that informal procedures are optional.

    The formal student complaint process for peer sexual harassment needs to be congruent with other related policies such as codes of conduct, student and personnel handbooks and regulations, including those concerning discipline, disability, and race discrimination. The latter two are particularly important because often more than one form of discrimination is involved, as in simultaneously taunting a student with a racial or ethnic slur *and* a sexual word. Just as district-wide policy on discrimination can cover discrimination on the basis of race, sex, nationality and ethnicity, religion, physical disability and sexual orientation, the sexual harassment policy can cover other forms of harassment as well.

Formal complaint procedures may vary among primary, middle school, and high school as established by the district. In general, the policy should answer these questions about the complaint process:

- Who handles complaints? In addition to the sexual harassment administrator who oversees the handling of all complaints (and who is often the person in charge of prevention and training efforts), one person in each school and site should be responsible for sexual harassment issues, to ensure that the policy is followed, time frames are observed, and questions from all parties are answered.

- Who decides to pursue a complaint? The district should be able to pursue a complaint without waiting for a formal or informal complaint from a student or family member.
- Can a person who observes sexual harassment (a third party) file a complaint? Often students who are not directly harassed may be affected by the harassment and should be able to bring their own complaint.
- Can family members file a complaint on behalf of their child? As "agents" for their minor children, family members should be allowed to do so.
- What are the time frames for filing and responding to a formal complaint? The time frame for filing a complaint should not be less than 180 days, which is the federal requirement for filing a charge under Title IX. If the time frame for filing an internal complaint is less than 180 days and has expired before the internal complaint could have been filed, the smaller time frame can have the unintended effect of leaving families with no option but to file a complaint with the federal government or to bring a lawsuit. Time limits should be able to be extended with good reason, for example, if the student was seriously incapacitated, there was a death in the family, etc.
- What is the family notification process? Who is notified, when, and by whom?
- When is an investigation to begin and how soon must it be completed?
- Who conducts the investigation? What are the guidelines for investigating a formal complaint?
- What is the standard of proof? Unlike a criminal investigation where the standard of proof is "beyond any reasonable doubt," the standard of proof in a school administrative proceeding is typically "the preponderance of evidence." That standard is: given the preponderance of evidence, a reasonable person would agree that the behavior happened or did not happen and that the sexual harassment policy was violated.

- What is the time frame for results of the investigation to be transmitted to the decision authority?
- Who decides whether a student violated or did not violate the policy? In some instances the person(s) doing the investigation makes that decision; in other instances, the investigator presents the information to the decision authority, who makes the decision as to whether the policy was violated.
- Does the investigation include recommendations to the decision authority or does the decision authority act without recommendations from the investigator?
- Who decides the penalty, if any?
- How soon are decisions made about sanctions? Ideally the investigation and recommendations should be completed within two weeks.
- How soon must the decision be communicated to the student who brought the charges, to the student who was charged with violating the policy, to their teachers, and to their families?
- Is there an appeal process and if so, does it include time frames and a clearly defined process?

It is helpful to include, as an appendix to the policy, a list of articles, books, and videos, and where they are readily available, such as at school libraries, guidance office, nurse's office, and principal's and district offices. The policy should also be included in the district website. School-specific websites should have a link to the sexual harassment policy on the district website.

NOTES

1. Told to author.
2. Materials in this chapter were adapted from "Elements of a Good Policy," by Bernice R. Sandler, in *Sexual Harassment on Campus: A Guide for Administrators, Faculty and Students*, edited by Bernice R. Sandler and Robert J. Shoop (Boston: Allyn and Bacon, 1996), pp. 104–27.

CHAPTER 4

How to Develop and Implement an Ongoing Training Program

A policy indicates a formal commitment made by the institution to end sexual harassment. The best-written policy is worthless, however, if it is not followed by dissemination, implementation, training, and evaluation. The next two chapters deal with training and dissemination.

Use this chapter to develop an effective and comprehensive training program for staff at all levels. It covers:

What Training Programs Should Accomplish
Who Is in Charge of Training
Who Conducts the Training
Who Needs to Be Trained
Records of Training
How to Evaluate the Training
Sample Training Outline
Useful Handouts for Training
Planning an Introductory Sexual Harassment Meeting for Staff at the
    School Level

Although 69 percent of students report that schools have a policy to deal with sexual harassment, and more than a third (36 percent) say that their schools distribute booklets, handouts, and other literature and materials about sexual harassment, only 9 percent of students report that their schools deal effectively with this issue.[1]

A training program to educate all school personnel is essential. A well-written comprehensive policy still requires training for its component parts to be understood and implemented. Increasingly school systems are adapting policies prohibiting student-to-student harassment, but few have conducted effective training programs. Many schools have implemented training as a one-time event, rather than as an ongoing process.

Administrators, including principals and the sexual harassment ad-minstrator for the district, as well as the site complaint managers, should receive formal training at least annually; other personnel should receive training at least every two years. The more knowledge that staff have about sexual harassment, the more likely they will be prepared to pre-vent it and to respond effectively when it occurs.

Training for students is critical. The American Association of Uni-versity Women (AAUW) 2001 study found that 96 percent of the high school students knew what sexual harassment was, yet 54 per-cent said that they had sexually harassed someone during their school lives.[2]

Student suggestions for improving their school's handling of sexual harassment issues:

"[Schools can] have teachers watch more closely to monitor for sexual harassment because sometimes they see it but don't care."

"Anything but show videos."

"Instead of popping in a video and expecting the problem to be solved, teachers need to take time out and TALK to us. It's a problem that one video can't fix."

"Have teachers teach more about it and not just blow off complaints."[3]

Although some training is often conducted at the school level, the district is ultimately responsible for the design and implementation of training programs and coordinating and working directly with schools in developing and carrying out schools' training and awareness pro-grams. Training can be included at in-service training or at ongoing staff meetings.

With protocols in place to deal with sexual harassment, teachers can suc-cessfully support a disclosing student, instead of unwittingly adding to her distress.[4]

WHAT TRAINING PROGRAMS SHOULD ACCOMPLISH

After training, participants should be able to:

- Support the district's strong commitment to prevent and respond to sexual harassment.
- Recognize the behaviors that constitute sexual harassment, including examples of computer harassment.
- Recognize the behaviors that constitute retaliation.
- Understand the moral, legal, educational, social, and emotional implications of student-to-student harassment.
- Know the essential information contained in the policy, including the necessary steps to be instituted when a sexual harassment incident is reported.
- Know how to respond if a child or adult reports a sexual harassment incident and to whom the person should be referred.
- Accept the responsibility to report all incidents and know how and to whom it should be reported.
- Be able to intervene when sexual harassment is observed (especially for teachers, administrators, and principals).
- Know where to obtain additional information.
- Know what records must be kept and how to keep them.

WHO IS IN CHARGE OF TRAINING

The person designated to be in charge of sexual harassment for the district is usually in charge of sexual harassment training. If there is a separate training unit within the district, the designated person should coordinate with that unit.

WHO CONDUCTS THE TRAINING

The person in charge of sexual harassment training for the district may also conduct training. If outside experts are hired for training, the sexual harassment administrator should play a major role in the development of

the agenda for training programs. Additionally each school should designate a site complaint manager to be in charge of sexual harassment issues
(sometimes the principal or vice principal) who may conduct additional
training at the school. The sexual harassment administrator should provide assistance, information, and resources to each school.

WHO NEEDS TO BE TRAINED

All staff, administrators, teachers, aides, nurses, counselors, coaches, police liaison officers, and nonprofessional staff such as office staff, physical plant personnel, cafeteria workers, bus drivers, security guards, and
volunteers—in short, *everyone* who is likely to have regular or occasional
contact with students or is in a position to observe them—needs training.
Additionally, families and community organizations should also be informed about sexual harassment. (See chapter 8 for a description of community and family programs.)

All employees should receive the same basic information described
earlier in this chapter.

Specialized training should also be conducted for the following
groups:

- Principals, vice principals, supervisors, and other administrators
  will need more specific information about the policy including:
  —district and personal liability
  —detailed information about their role in implementing the policy,
    including training at the site level
  —handling of complaints and retaliation, including follow-up
  —reporting procedures and record keeping
  —incorporating sexual harassment as subject matter in other re-
    lated ongoing programs such as peer mediation, character de-
    velopment, violence and bullying prevention, conflict manage-
    ment, and anger management programs
  —utilizing informal and formal procedures in responding to re-
    ports of peer sexual harassment
- Teachers will need additional information about:
  —how to intervene when they observe sexual harassment

- —how to respond to student reports of sexual harassment and retaliation
- —how to conduct discussions about sexual harassment in their classroom
- —how to create a positive environment and reward good behavior
- —reporting procedures and record keeping
- —utilizing informal procedures
- —helping victims and harassers
- —incorporating sexual harassment as subject matter in other related programs such as peer mediation, character development, and bullying prevention
- —how to respond to computer harassment
- • Professional staff such as nurses, guidance counselors, and others who may be contacted by students who experience or observe sexual harassment need additional information on:
  - —how to respond to reports of sexual harassment and retaliation
  - —reporting procedures
  - —record keeping
- • Complaint managers at the building level need additional information on how to help:
  - —students who have been harassed and their families
  - —students who harass and their families
  - —teachers dealing with students involved in sexual harassment
  - —teachers dealing with an entire class or other group when appropriate
  - —bystanders, staff, or students, to respond more actively when harassment occurs
- • Substitute and student teachers need information about recognizing sexual harassment, responding to it effectively, and keeping appropriate records.
- • Coaches should receive training. They are strong role models for athletes. Students may be more likely to confide in them about peer harassment. Additionally, some student athletes may be more likely to harass other students. Coaches need information about:
  - —recognizing harassment
  - —how to respond to reports of sexual harassment
  - —reporting procedures and record keeping

  —how to intervene when they observe sexual harassment
  —how to conduct discussions about harassment with their ath-
    letes.
- Computer staff need additional information on
  —how to identify computer harassment including peer harassment
    on school and home computers including e-mail, instant mes-
    saging, and individual websites
  —how to respond to complaints of computer harassment and re-
    taliation on both school and home computers
  —reporting procedures
  —record keeping
  —how to integrate peer harassment issues into existing rules and
    training on computer use
- Nonprofessional staff, such as office staff, cafeteria workers, bus
  drivers, crossing guards, security guards, physical plant personnel,
  and playground supervisors need additional information about:
  —how to respond when they observe sexual harassment or when
    it is reported to them
  —when and how to intervene
  —reporting procedures and requirements
- Volunteers and aides will need additional information on:
  —how to respond when they observe sexual harassment and when
    it is reported to them
  —when and how to intervene
  —reporting procedures and record keeping
- New personnel need information about sexual harassment in their
  orientation program as well as receiving the same formal training
  given to other employees. Simply describing sexual harassment
  and the policy in the employee handbook and distributing printed
  materials and/or viewing a video is not sufficient training.
- Students at all levels need information about:
  —what student-to-student sexual harassment is
  —how to respond to it whether it happens to them or another stu-
    dent
  —to whom to report the incident
  —how complaints of harassment and retaliation are handled
  —prohibition against retaliation

Students working part-time should be reminded that if they experience sexual harassment on the job they may be able to obtain helpful information from the site complaint manager. (If the workplace harassment involved other students, the school could intervene directly.)

Training for students is almost always best conducted at the building level. Formal training and information should be part of the orientation process for students entering middle and high school. New or transfer students and their families also need information about sexual harassment in their orientation information. In addition to training for all students, further training for high school leaders and athletes may be of value, with a focus on prevention and intervention.

Although some schools offer "bully-prevention programs," they often fail to include sexual harassment as a form of bullying. At a bullying conference for school personnel, one of the authors asked a middle school girl and a high school boy if they thought it was bullying if a guy continually touched a girl's breasts even though the girl indicated that she wanted the boy to stop.

The middle school girl said that the behavior was not bullying but was sexual harassment. The high school boy also said that the behavior was not bullying and added that "boys had certain needs and desires."

Thus both students did not view sexual bullying, that is, sexual harassment, as related to bullying. Consequently, it is not likely that they will incorporate or extend what they learned about bullying into their feelings and behaviors about sexual harassment.[5]

RECORDS OF TRAINING

To ensure that coverage has been complete, keep records about:

- Training content
- Attendees, including job title and department
- A list of those who missed the training and who will need to be scheduled for a future training session
- Date and length of training
- Place
- Name of trainer(s)

- Copies of handouts
- Evaluations
- Summary of problems encountered, if any
- Follow-up needed, if any
- Future directions

A summary of the training conducted should appear in the annual report.

HOW TO EVALUATE THE TRAINING

Evaluation is important not only to assess the quality of training but to gauge its impact and to recognize needs for additional training and/or information. Each participant should receive an evaluation form at the end of the training session or at the end of particular segments. (Time to fill out the form should be included in the training schedule.) Questions about the content and about the training process, such as the following, should be included:

	Yes	No
Do you understand the main points of the training?	____	____
(areas of training can be listed separately)		
Do you understand what your responsibilities are?	____	____
Was the speaker clear?	____	____
Were the handouts clear?	____	____
What information do you need now?		

(Additional questions about the training process should also be included.)

SAMPLE TRAINING OUTLINE

The outline below can be modified to take into account previous training, new issues, and the needs of particular groups. Sections will vary in presentation and time, depending on the position of the employees being trained, previous training, and current issues. Administrators need to know relatively more about the legal implications; physical plant personnel may need to know less about intervening and more about reporting. Approximately three to six hours are needed to cover the agenda, depending on the amount of interactive exercises included.

1. Student-to-student sexual harassment: what it is and what it isn't
   a. Definition
   b. Example
   c. Impact of sexual harassment
   d. Incidence of harassment, including national and local data. (Many people are often unaware of the extent of peer sexual harassment. It is therefore helpful to gather some data and information about student-to-student sexual harassment in the particular school or the district prior to the training. For information on how to gather local information, see "How to Assess the Extent of Peer Harassment in the District and School Environments" in chapter 3.)
2. Why does sexual harassment occur?
   a. Myths about sexual harassment
   b. Harassment and power: using sexuality to intimidate others
   c. Flirting and sexual harassment
   d. Confusion between friendliness and sexuality.
3. Legal ramifications: Training sessions that focus heavily on the legal aspects of sexual harassment are generally not as productive as those which focus on other issues such as employee obligations and interventions. For most staff, the section on legal ramifications should be short, focusing on these points:
   a. Sexual harassment violates federal and state laws such as Title IX of the Education Amendments Act, Title VII of the Civil Rights Act, and state sexual abuse and sexual assault laws.
   b. Individuals and institutions can be held legally liable for sexual harassment charges that are not responded to or handled effectively.
   c. When physical behaviors are involved, state criminal sexual assault and abuse laws may apply and *must* be reported to designated authorities.

4. District policy concerning student-to-student sexual harassment:
   a. Relationship of policy to participants' responsibilities and obligations
      i)   responsibility of district and its employees to prevent and respond to student-to-student sexual harassment
      ii) responsibility of all personnel to take sexual harassment incidents seriously
      iii) responsibility of all personnel to report incidents to the appropriate designated person
      iv) responsibility to intervene when student-to-student harassment is observed: what interventions are effective and the application of appropriate discipline
   b. Other policy issues
      i)   confidentiality policy, including those who "need to know" and those who do not
      ii) prohibition against retaliation and reprisals against anyone who reports sexual harassment behavior
      iii) same-sex harassment
      iv) multiple harassment issues: sexual harassment and race and/or disability and/or same-sex harassment
      v)   consensual relationships
      vi) false charges
5. Informal and formal ways of dealing with complaints
   a. Advantages and disadvantages of formal and informal procedures
      i)   the formal complaint process
           (1) how it works
           (2) standard of evidence
      ii) informal ways of handling complaints
           (1) what institutions can do
           (2) what victims can do
6. Where additional information can be obtained
7. Information about future meetings or training sessions

USEFUL HANDOUTS FOR TRAINING

Training can be implemented and enhanced by effective handouts. Handouts should cover the following issues:

- A copy of the policy and/or a simplified summary of it (and where to obtain a complete copy)
- A list of examples of sexual harassment
- How sexual harassment affects students
- A brief summary of laws covering sexual harassment
- How to respond when someone tells you that they have been harassed (a sample script is helpful)
- How not to respond when someone tells you that they have been harassed
- How to respond when someone tells you that they saw someone else being harassed
- A description of ways to intervene (sample scripts are critical)
- How to report incidents of sexual harassment and retaliation, and to whom
- A list of resources available in the school and/or the district

Sections from this book, including the appendixes, may be used as handouts, provided credit includes the authors, title, and publisher.

PLANNING AN INTRODUCTORY SEXUAL HARASSMENT MEETING FOR STAFF AT THE SCHOOL LEVEL

Whether or not sexual harassment is a new issue in the school, the principal should convene a required introductory meeting for all school staff on peer sexual harassment. More than one session may be necessary, depending on school size and need to accommodate different schedules and different groups. The purpose of this meeting is to help all staff understand what sexual harassment is, its impact on all students, the strong commitment of school and district to prevent sexual harassment, and how to respond properly when it occurs. This meeting can serve as the first part of the formal training program on sexual harassment. The agenda may be drawn from the sample outline presented earlier in this chapter.

Attendees should include all classroom and special teachers, computer personnel, office staff, volunteers, guidance personnel, coaches, cafeteria staff, physical plant staff, and security personnel. Separate meetings may be conducted for the different groups. Regular staff meetings can be used for these meetings. *Persons who do not attend this meeting should be re-quired to attend a similar meeting at either another school or at one con-ducted by the district.* Everyone in the district should receive the training, whether conducted at the school or district level.

In order to begin developing a wide base of support, the principal should plan this meeting with a school committee on sexual harass-ment. District staff assigned to work with sexual harassment issues should also be consulted on the content of the meeting and to provide resources and information to the planners. If possible, district staff should be invited to the training session as resource persons. A separate meeting for families and community members should also be con-ducted. (A "Sample Agenda for Sexual Harassment Meeting with Fam-ilies" appears in chapter 8.

NOTES

1. *Hostile Hallways: Bullying, Teasing, and Sexual Harassment in School* (Washington, D.C.: American Association of University Women, Educational Foundation, 2001), pp. 15, 17.

2. *Hostile Hallways*, p. 5.

3. *Hostile Hallways*, pp. 9, 17.

4. L. Walls, "Bullying and Sexual Harassment in Schools," n.d. Retrieved June 26, 2004, from www.children.org/article_walls1_stmL

5. Told to author.

CHAPTER 5

Next Steps: How to Let Everyone Know about Student-to-Student Sexual Harassment

The critical components in the success of any antiharassment program are helping staff, students, and their families understand what peer harassment is; their individual responsibility; and the district's commitment to prevent and stop it. In addition to formal training, disseminating information is a useful way to help members of the school community learn about sexual harassment and to reinforce what they have already learned.

Use this chapter for strategies to provide information to staff, students, and community:

How to Disseminate the Policy
How to Help Students Understand Student-to-Student Sexual Harassment
Breaking the Code of Silence

HOW TO DISSEMINATE THE POLICY

Although the district is ultimately responsible to oversee the development and dissemination of information, individual schools may also supplement the district's efforts with activities of their own. The following checklist will help districts and schools facilitate everyone's understanding.

- Develop an information and dissemination program using print resources, school mail, e-mail, and a website to educate and periodically remind personnel, students, and families about sexual harassment.

- Distribute the new, revised, or current sexual harassment policy or a summary at least annually, as well as a letter about sexual harassment, to all employees to remind them of the district's commitment to end such harassment and to remind them about what is required of them. Use school mail or e-mail.
- Distribute the policy, the policy summary, and a letter about sexual harassment annually (such as at the beginning of the school year) to all students and their families.
- Include a letter or statement from the superintendent and/or the board of education to emphasize the importance of the issues.
- Develop a short summary of the policy and/or other materials in an easy-to-read format, such as a brochure that older students and adults can understand. (In some instances a special summary aimed at students is helpful.) These materials should include the following:
  —a definition and examples of sexual harassment
  —personnel responsibilities
  —student responsibilities
  —informal and formal handling of complaints, including an example of each
  —whom to tell about incidents
  —where to obtain additional information (name of person, office and phone number)
  —where to obtain a copy of the policy
  —a list of frequently asked questions and answers
- Post these materials on the district website. They may be included on individual school websites or alternatively, these sites should provide links to these materials on the district's site.
- Distribute the same or similar materials to families at least annually, with a similar accompanying letter or e-mail, listing where a copy of the policy can be obtained. Information in chapter 8, such as "How Families Can Discuss Sexual Harassment with Their Child" and a "Sample Letter to Families about Sexual Harassment" can be included.

- Make the summaries easily available on a year-round basis in designated district and school offices, including:
  —all administrators' offices
  —teacher lounges
  —library
  —nurse's and counselor's offices
- Periodically distribute summaries and other materials available at school meetings for teachers and families and at PTA meetings.
- Include the policy or its summary in the Employee and Student Handbooks.
- Include the summary in the district telephone directory and in other printed matter.
- Reference the policy in union contracts and affirmative action plans.
- When revisions occur, no matter how minor, inform everyone. A revised policy demonstrates that harassment is not a static issue and will be reviewed periodically.
- Distribute written materials to teachers (in addition to their training) to provide guidance on how to discuss the policy with their students, appropriate to the students' age.
- Post and disseminate a list of resources for staff and families, including articles, books, and videos available from the school library and other school offices.
- Include the name, location, phone number, fax, and e-mail of the person to contact about sexual harassment on all materials relating to the issue.
- Post sexual harassment materials on the district website, as well as references to these materials on individual school sites.
- Prepare and distribute an annual report on sexual harassment. (See "What to Include in Annual Reports" in appendix A.)
- Both the superintendent and principals should periodically send out to staff, students, and families information and materials about peer sexual harassment and related school activities, ongoing training, articles, and other information.
- Send a letter to all families about the district's policy on sexual harassment, including information on how it will be handled both

formally and informally. Other materials for families and communities are described in chapter 8.

- When serious incidents occur, principals and/or the superintendent may find it useful to let all students and their families know what has happened and how the district has responded. This information helps educate everyone about how the district's commitment to protect students is being implemented. It reassures students and their families that incidents are being handled quickly and effectively, and builds trust in the district's ability to stop harassment.
- Inform, annually in writing, all teachers and staff about how all incidents should be reported and to whom.
- Inform, annually in writing, administrators of student-job-training sites about the policy, and how all incidents should be reported and to whom.
- Inform, annually in writing, all student teachers and their supervisors about the policy against sexual harassment, and require them to report any incidents they observe.
- Inform, annually in writing, all vendors, contractors, and salespersons who visit or work at schools about the policy against sexual harassment, and ask them to report any instances they observe. Include the name and phone number of the office or person to whom such incidents should be reported.
- Keep records of materials disseminated to staff, students, families, and others. These records should be kept at both the district and school level.
- Develop a comprehensive website about sexual harassment, posting the policy, a summary, resources, persons to contact, district and school activities, information for families, articles, cartoons, etc. Many schools provide a book with the school schedule and other related information. Rules about sexual harassment should be included.
- Publicize the district's efforts to prevent sexual harassment. Send out press releases including information on sexual harassment prevention programs.

Keep records of all materials disseminated, including a description, date, and recipient list.

HOW TO HELP STUDENTS UNDERSTAND
STUDENT-TO-STUDENT SEXUAL HARASSMENT

In addition to easy-to-read summary material about the policy and specialized training for students, other activities can also help in increasing student awareness. Some of these activities could be conducted on either the district or school level, such as the following:

- Support the development of a district-wide code of behavior that encourages respect among students, including consequences for breaking the rules. A Student Bill of Rights might include:
  —Everyone has the right to feel safe at school.
  —No one has the right to verbally or physically hurt or touch other students in ways that make them feel uncomfortable.
  —No one has the right to threaten someone with physical harm or social consequences if they report an incident.
- Post the Student Bill of Rights throughout the school and district as well as sending it out to personnel and families.
- Conduct an assembly, speak-out, or conference about sexual harassment annually at the district or school level. *Involve students* in presenting information, developing skits, etc. This is a good way to increase staff and student morale and to make all proud of their school. Invite district leaders, school board members, and families.
- Post and disseminate a list of resources for students, including books and videos in the school libraries dealing with sexual harassment. Encourage the library office to purchase such materials.
- Display student-made posters and banners about respect and sexual harassment so that attractive artwork about sexual harassment issues can be posted throughout the district in offices, classrooms, bathrooms, hallways, stairways, cafeteria, gym, schoolyard, buses, and library. To avoid overtly sexual posters, provide guidelines about what the posters can include. If appropriate, conduct a poster contest about sexual harassment among students.
- Encourage students to form an organization or club to focus on sexual harassment issues and provide a staff person to recruit members, both male and female, and to work with the group by providing ideas, resources, and guidance for group activities.

- Provide training about sexual harassment.
- Pass out bookmarks that contain a definition of sexual harassment and where to get help.
- Students can be required to read the sexual harassment rules posted on the school or district website. They should also be required to sign a form saying they have done so, stating that they understand the rules and will abide by them. Students can read the rules on their home computers or on the school computer by requesting to go on the Internet.
- When possible, have students develop materials about student-to-student sexual harassment, for example, a video demonstrating appropriate behaviors on school buses.
- Develop materials on free speech and sexual harassment. (See chapter 2.)
- Develop a "No Name-Calling Week" as a way of calling attention to sexual harassment and bullying. (This is most appropriate for elementary grades.)[1]

BREAKING THE CODE OF SILENCE

Many students never tell *anyone* that they have been sexually harassed. They worry about what might happen if they complain about a fellow student; they worry about retaliation; and often they have accepted the common taboo that "snitching" or "ratting" on your "friends" or getting them in trouble is not acceptable.

Students need help in understanding that there is a difference between simply "telling on another student" just to get them in trouble, and *protecting oneself or someone else from harm.*

Here are some actions schools can take to help students understand this distinction and to break the code of silence:

- Conduct an assembly where the distinction between "snitching" and reporting is discussed, perhaps as part of a student skit.
  - Stress the responsibility that everyone has to report activities that hurt other people or damage property, such as vandalism, theft, threats, physical harm, bullying, racial harassment, and sexual harassment.

- —Distinguish between activities that hurt people and property and other actions, such as chewing gum or passing notes.
- —Inform students whom they should tell, such as the school complaint manager, the vice principal, a counselor, or a designated teacher. Explain how confidentiality is respected and what steps the school will take to protect a student against retaliation.
- —Allow time for discussion and for follow-up discussion with teachers.
- Incorporate information about the distinction between snitching and reporting in all sexual harassment training that is aimed at students.
- Conduct a student poster contest. Developing posters encourages reporting. For example, a poster with the words: "TELL SOME-ONE" containing a list of behaviors and a list of people whom to tell. Other posters could describe the policy about retaliation and confidentiality.
- Develop multiple ways for students to report sexual harassment they observe or experience, such as
  - —telling or writing a teacher
  - —telling or writing the site complaint manager or the sexual harassment coordinator
  - —telling or writing the principal, vice principal, nurse, counselor
  - —telling their family and asking them to contact the school
  - —calling the school hotline
- Conduct classroom discussions around the issue of reporting and why it is important.
- Send home materials to families encouraging them to talk with their children about the importance of telling them and the school about harassment when they see it happening or when it happens to them.
- Develop ways to help students understand what happens when someone complains, such as using skits, handouts, posters, and discussion.
- Develop ways to inform students how actual complaints have been handled. This is especially important when the behavior is egregious and known to many students. If privacy considerations make this difficult, students can at least be informed that discipline was invoked, that the school is very concerned about what happened, and is taking steps to see that this behavior does not occur again.

Using a "Let's Talk about It" Box

A "Let's Talk about It" box can be used in primary grades to encourage students to identify problems that need to be discussed by the class and teacher. Often the teacher is unaware of the problems raised, such as teasing. The box provides a safe way for students to tell teachers about others who are behaving badly toward them or toward others. Students should be encouraged to also report sexual harassing behaviors, which can result in teacher discussion and other actions as needed. Students can sign their name or report anonymously. See "Anonymous Complaints" in appendix B. A similar box in middle and high schools could be used for reporting school problems, with students encouraged to also report sexual harassment. Students can be encouraged to report incidents in groups; a student need not report alone to the teacher or other adult. (See "What to Do When Students Ask You Not to Tell Anyone Else" in chapter 6.)

NOTE

1. The No Name-Calling Week Project (created by GLSEN and Simon and Schuster Children's Publishing) consists of a coalition of more than forty national partner organizations. It is targeted to grades 5–8. For further information, see www.nonamecallingweek.org.

What to Do When Peer Harassment Occurs: Practices and Procedures

How adults respond when harassment occurs is the core of any sexual harassment program. No matter how comprehensive the written policy, no matter how extensive the training and dissemination, no matter what programs are conducted, if adults do not know how to respond appropriately when sexual harassment occurs, those initiatives will not accomplish positive change. The climate, in large measure, will depend on how sexual harassment incidents are dealt with when they occur.

In this chapter you will find effective strategies to intervene and respond to sexual harassment incidents:

Why It Is Important to Respond and Intervene When Peer Sexual Harassment Occurs
How to Handle a Complaint When You Don't Know What to Do
Principles of Intervention
How to Help Students Who Are Harassed
How to Help Students Who Harass
How to Handle Sexual Harassment Complaints
Sample Letters of Resolution
How to Deal with Video and Computer Harassment

> Often dismissed as adolescent pranks, rites of passage, or awkward attempts at sexual teasing, sexual harassment is seldom interrupted by the very adults who are in a position to advocate for respectful treatment of all students. Even when sexual harassment is addressed, intervention seldom occurs at an institutional level . . . even the most concerned teachers often deal with harassment, even by chronic offenders, privately and on a case-by-case basis. The result is that both girls and boys witness

sexist, racist, and homophobic behavior being displayed publicly, in front of adults and peers, without repercussion.[1]

In English class, right in front of the teacher, Joey will say, "I think I'm getting hard" when his girlfriend walks in or when he wants to embarrass some girl. The teacher only says, "Joey, calm down." Joey will say to girls, "I want you now." He does this to the unpopular girls to embarrass them and make them feel uncomfortable. Everybody laughs at the girl. She blushes or walks away.[2]

WHY IT IS IMPORTANT TO RESPOND AND INTERVENE WHEN PEER SEXUAL HARASSMENT OCCURS

Every time an adult does not speak out or intervene when witnessing the bullying or harassment of a student, they are complicit in that abuse.[3]

With protocols in place to deal with sexual harassment, teachers can successfully support a disclosing student, instead of unwittingly adding to her distress.[4]

Educators frequently find it difficult to intervene when they observe a student being treated in a sexually harassing manner. They may not know what to say. Perhaps they believe that it is none of their business, or they do not know how best to intervene. They may believe that students are best left to their own devices to solve whatever conflicts arise among them. They may not understand that they have both an educational and legal obligation to intervene whenever a student is intimidating someone in a sexual manner.

Ten-year-old LaShonda Davis was continually propositioned by her eleven-year-old fifth-grade classmate, G. F., who sat next to her. He told her he wanted to have sex with her on several occasions. His behavior included obscene gestures and language, repeated threats, attempted and actual touching of LaShonda's breasts and vaginal areas, and making sexual sounds and actions. LaShonda told her teacher almost every time the behavior happened. The school refused to change LaShonda's seat for three months.

Her mother, Mrs. Davis, complained to the teacher after almost every time the behavior happened. She also contacted the principal, the Superintendent, the Board of Education, the state's Professional Practices Commission, and the Department of Family and Children's Services. None made any attempt to stop the behavior. When Mrs. Davis finally complained to the Monroe County Sheriff's office, G.F. was charged with and pled guilty to sexual battery.

Mrs. Davis then sued the school District under Title IX. The Supreme Court agreed that Title IX did cover student-to-student sexual harassment. The case was finally settled with an undisclosed amount paid to LaShonda Davis by the District.[5]

By *not* responding to observed sexual harassment, adults may inadvertently convey a message of approval, thus implying that the behavior is acceptable and not offensive. The message may also convey that the adult is too weak to intervene and stop the behavior or simply does not care. Whatever the reason, students are likely to feel unsafe and less likely to trust those adults and possibly others in the school.

Dangerous Words: How Not to Respond to a Report or Complaint of Sexual Harassment

Many people—administrators, teachers, and other employees—often downplay or deny the existence of sexual harassment. Instead of dealing with it, seeking more information, or referring a complaint to someone who can handle it, they may dismiss complaints with phrases such as those listed below. In addition to ignoring a plea for help, these responses can expose the school and staff to possible liability. A student or family hearing such words in response to their complaints of sexual harassment may be discouraged from complaining any further or give up on the school as a source of help. Instead, they may seek redress from state or federal enforcement agencies or the courts. Many of the comments listed below were drawn from charges filed against schools. Unhelpful and dangerous words such as the following should be avoided:

- It's just teasing—no big deal.
- I know that he [she] didn't mean anything like that.
- John is such a great kid, I know he would never do that.

- If you girls didn't dress like that, there wouldn't be any sexual harassment.
- When you grow up and go to work you'll need to learn to handle things like that.
- Just ignore it. It's no big deal.
- Stay away from those boys.
- He puts his arms around everyone; he's just being friendly.
- He (she) really likes you, that's why he (she) is doing it (behaving badly, being mean, etc.).
- He's all boy.
- He's just standing up for himself.
- Don't be such a wimp. You're old enough to stand up for yourself.
- You're overreacting.
- Don't be such a prude.
- Don't tattle.
- It's just a prank—where's your sense of humor?
- It's just a prank that got out of hand.
- What did you expect after telling everyone you are gay [or lesbian]?
- You don't want to get him into trouble, do you?
- Why don't you develop a sense of humor?
- You must have wanted it—otherwise you should have told him "no."
- The boys (girls) are just being rude and childish.
- Don't worry about it—they're not serious.
- You have to understand he is from a different culture.
- We certainly would deal with it but no one wants to file a complaint so our hands are tied.
- With her disability, I just don't believe anyone would be sexually bothering her.
- No one else ever complained about this before.
- Boys and girls are going to bother each other, tease each other, and fool around. To call that sexual harassment is going too far.
- It's part of growing up. You have to learn how to deal with it.
- It's not really sexual harassment. It's just a failure of communication. It's just offensive behavior.

- If we had to discipline every student who used bad language we wouldn't have time for anything else.
- Boys will be boys.
- Girls will be girls.

(Excerpted from materials written by Bernice R. Sandler for *Educator's Guide to Controlling Sexual Harassment* [Washington, D.C.: Thompson Publishing Group, 1993]. Additional material included.)

HOW TO HANDLE A COMPLAINT
WHEN YOU DON'T KNOW WHAT TO DO

Handling a sexual harassment complaint is difficult and requires both training and experience. What should you do if a student comes to you and describes behaviors that may be sexually harassing, and you don't know what to do? The following steps may be especially helpful to those who are not in a position to intervene directly or have no direct responsibility for the student.

1. Show concern. "I'm sorry this is happening to you."
2. Take the report seriously. Don't use "dangerous words" such as those listed above.
3. Tell the student that the district has a policy: "We have a policy that prohibits this kind of behavior and deals with this kind of problem."
4. Refer the complaint to the proper staff person. Know the name of the person who handles sexual harassment complaints at both the school and district level. "I'm not the best person to talk to about this. Ms. Marks has lots of experience with this and has helped a lot of people like you. Let me call her right now and see when she can see you. If you would like me to go with you, I will."
5. Provide for follow-up. "If that doesn't work out, get back to me and we'll figure out what to do next." Call or seek out the student during the next few days. Find out whether the student talked to the appropriate person, whether the harassment has stopped, and whether any additional action is needed.

6. Keep a written record of the student's remarks and your response.

(Based on "How to Handle a Sexual Harassment Complaint: Passing the Hot Potato to Someone Else," by Bernice Sandler, in *About Women on Campus*, newsletter of the National Association for Women in Education [now defunct], Spring 1994, pp. 5–6.)

PRINCIPLES OF INTERVENTION

Ways to intervene and respond to sexual harassment are provided below, along with examples:

- Accept a student's appraisal that she or he is upset. Sometimes there is a marked difference in the way in which a student and an adult may view an incident. Even if it does not look like a serious event for the adult, it is serious for the student. Students are the best judges of what is upsetting to them.
- Do not blame the student who is being harassed; the fault lies with the person doing the harassing.
- Intervene immediately when the offensive behavior occurs. If you do not want to address the behavior publicly, you can still intervene. Immediately address the student who behaved offensively, and set up a specific time to talk to the student, using language such as, "I need to talk you after class today. You need to stay here when the class ends." This message tells other students that the behavior was out of line and that appropriate action will be taken.
- Describe or name the behavior observed. Be precise, firm, and direct.
- State that this behavior must stop immediately.
- Provide a strong warning with future consequences as written in the school policy or code of behavior. If the behavior has occurred previously, invoke the consequence without further warning.

    Examples:

    You are making sexual comments and causing Susan to feel hurt. This needs to stop right now. If this continues, you will be sent to the vice principal immediately and your family will be notified. This behavior must stop immediately.

This comment is offensive to all of us, not just to me alone. It violates the school's sexual harassment policy (or code of behavior). This behavior has to stop. We respect each other in this classroom. You signed the code of behavior, and you need to read it aloud right now, understand it, and learn what the consequences are for continuing this behavior.

Calling someone names is a put-down and is not acceptable here. This kind of behavior is not allowed in our school because it hurts people and we care for people. You need to apologize to Mary right now.

This is not the first time you have said things like this and it is a form of sexual harassment. There are consequences for hurting other people physically or verbally and I have told you before what they are. I am sending you to the vice principal right now. We also need to talk about why you engage in this behavior. I also will set up an appointment for you to meet with the guidance counselor.

- Use the incident as an opportunity to discuss it with the class at that moment.

  Michael just said some very offensive things to Mary. That behavior is not allowed in this class. What does Michael need to understand? What can we do to help Mary?

- Do not ask the student who is the target of harassment to share her feelings about what happened, unless she volunteers to do so.
- Encourage the students to act on a valid suggestion, such as showing sympathy to Mary, or telling Michael to stop his behavior.
- Use language that focuses on the behavior, not on the person. Do not label the student as a sexual harasser or perpetrator, or attack the student personally.

  Calling students "sluts" or "whores" is sexual harassment, and is not allowed in our classroom [school].

- Include something positive about the student, to indicate that you like the student but not the behavior.

You are helpful to students in our classroom but when you make sexual jokes about other students and call them names like "fags," you are not helpful or caring, and you need to change this behavior.

- Do not use nonassertive language such as "Haven't I told you to stop that kind of behavior before?" or "How many times do I have to tell you not to use those words in school?"
- Read the school policy to the harassing student, or have the student read it aloud, including the appropriate consequences established in the code. Immediate consequences may include time-out, referral to a guidance counselor or administrator, or moving a student to another part of the room or to another room.
- Describe the student's harassing behavior and link it to the consequence.

   Bobby, I'm putting you on time-out because you called Tiffany some hurtful and sexual names, and that behavior isn't allowed. We respect each other in this classroom.

- Ask the student to state why he or she is being moved (or whatever consequence is initiated) to be sure the student understands why discipline is being invoked. Often students respond to this question by defending their actions instead of stating the reason for the consequence. When that occurs, repeat your description of the behavior and again tell the student why the consequence is being invoked.
- Require the harasser to apologize in writing or orally to the person harassed. The apology should include a description of what the behavior was and a promise to stop it (I'm sorry I called you a slut and I won't do it anymore). Insist that the apology is complete. Be sure that the harasser understands what the behavior is that needs to be stopped and describes this behavior in the apology. If the apology is a written note, read it before you or the harasser gives it to the student who was harassed. It is important for an adult to be present when the apology is given to show support for the person who was harassed and to be certain that the apology is not contaminated by hostile behavior or language by the student who is apologizing.

- Decide whether or not the behavior needs to be reported according to your school's policy. Criteria for reporting would include the seriousness of the behavior, and whether it is the first incident or reflects a pattern of continuing behavior, and how upset the student who was the object of the behavior is. Behaviors that include sexual touching are almost always a violation of state sexual abuse or sexual assault laws and should *always* be reported to the district as well as to the appropriate state authorities.
- Assess whether something needs to be done for the student(s) who was harassed and the student(s) who harassed. (See the sections that follow on "How to Help Students Who Are Harassed," and "How to Help Students Who Harass.")
  —Does the student who was the target of the harassment need reassurance that he or she is in a safe environment?
  —Tell the student to inform you (or the appropriate staff person) if harassment continues and/or whether there is any retaliation or threat of retaliation from the student who behaved badly or from other students.

  If anyone teases you or makes you feel bad about what happened or if anyone threatens you, let me or the vice principal know immediately and we will stop it. No one has a right to scare you.

  —Does either student need additional help, such as referral to counseling?
- Decide whether families need to be informed. This depends upon school policy. In general, the more severe or frequent the harassment, and the more upset the student is, the more important it is that the families of the harassed student, the harasser, and other students and their families be notified of the incident and informed of the actions taken. When in doubt, notify families.

  In notifying families emphasize that the families are a partner with the school and are encouraged to take positive steps for follow-up. The oral or written notification should occur quickly, preferably on the day the incident occurred, and should include:
  —what happened, when, and where
  —a statement noting that the behavior was a violation of school policy prohibiting peer harassment

—a description of how the school responded
—the consequences if the behavior recurs, and
—a description of follow-up plans.

- Families should be encouraged to contact the school for further information and support. If the notification is not in writing, a written description of the conversation should be made for the files, describing the information communicated. Often it is useful to follow up oral notification with a written one.
- The complaining student, accused student, and their families should be kept informed on the status of the complaints.
- Be certain, especially in the case of serious harassment or pervasive continual harassment, that the student being harassed understands the following:
  —It is not that student's fault.
  —The behavior that the other person engaged in was wrong.
  —The behavior violates district policy.
  —The school will not allow this kind of behavior.
  —The school is ready to help the student at all times.

> We are here to help you. We don't want you to face this alone. If there are any other problems, contact me or someone else to help.

- Keep records of all incidents, including retaliation, even if the behavior does not need to be reported. Records help assess the seriousness and frequency of a problem, providing an accurate account of how often incidents have occurred. They help in making the determination about whether a student will need additional help or interventions from other school personnel. These records can also help convince reluctant personnel and families to take action. Records should include:
  —date
  —place
  —what happened
  —who was present
  —how teachers and/or other staff responded
  —how the students involved reacted,
  —what the follow-up plans are (date implemented; by whom)

- Take all complaints about sexually harassing behaviors seriously whether from students, family members, or school personnel. Do not ignore behaviors by brushing them off as "boys will be boys" or "cultural differences." Even if a student is not upset by sexually harassing behavior, the incident still needs to be addressed.

  A Pittsburgh ninth-grade boy who pulled down the pants of another boy during gym class was suspended for three days. Although the targeted boy was reported as not being offended by the "prank" school officials viewed it differently. They also showed the class videos about sexual harassment and discussed the school's sexual harassment policy with them.[6]

- Treat boys and girls fairly. Sometimes schools treat girls more harshly than boys when sexual harassment occurs.

  In Texas, a group of football players mooned a group of cheerleaders who then mooned the boys back. The football players were suspended for three games; the cheerleaders were thrown off the squad.[7]

  Some behaviors by girls, such as spreading sexual rumors, may be ignored and labeled as "meanness" rather than as sexual harassment.

A Ten-Step Procedure for Responding to Incidents

1. Investigate the behavior if needed. Talk to each of the students involved separately in a private conversation. Advise the students involved in the incident(s) not to talk to each other until the incident(s) is resolved.
2. Ensure that the behavior stops.
3. Apply sanctions.
4. Notify family members where appropriate.
5. Keep records.
6. Assess other steps necessary for preventing a recurrence of the behavior.
7. Report the incident(s) to the site complaint manager.
8. Provide for social support for the victim, including family, and classmates.

9. Ensure that all follow-up plans are implemented.
10. Follow up with both students to ensure that the behavior has really stopped and that there is no retaliation from the harasser or from other students.

- When serious incidents of sexual harassment occur, respond quickly. Consider a public response. It is often difficult to conceal information successfully about serious incidents and it is better to deal with them openly. Not responding publicly is often viewed by students and the community at large as approval of the behavior or a lack of concern about what happened.

HOW TO HELP STUDENTS WHO ARE HARASSED

The students were sitting in a reading group. A boy opened his fly and rubbed his penis on the back of a girl sitting in front of him. The girl did not immediately realize what was happening and brushed her back several times while other students in back of her laughed. She finally turned around and was horrified. Although the boy was subsequently disciplined, no one from the school ever spoke to the girl about the incident. No one told her that the boy was disciplined or what the discipline was, or if the incident was even reported to anyone. No one ever told her that the incident was illegal and a violation of sexual assault law (and should have been reported). Her parents were not notified nor was the girl ever offered any help by the school. Nothing was said to other students, and several began to taunt her about the incident. Her grades dropped, she became fearful and withdrawn, developed eating and other problems, although previously she had shown no evidence of any problems (incident reported to one of the authors).

Many students who experience harassment often feel upset and fearful. They may not report harassing behaviors even if they feel overwhelmed by what is happening to them. How adults respond will affect how students will view the incident, including whether they will blame themselves, whether adults and the school will continue to be trusted, and whether the student will be able to feel safe again. The way incidents are handled will also affect whether other students will report sexual harassment incidents they experience or observe.

Guidelines for Interviewing Students Who Are Harassed

- Listen sympathetically and take all reports of sexual harassment from students and family members seriously.
- Be nonjudgmental in your questioning. Ask "What happened next?" rather than "What did you do to cause him to act that way?"
- Ask how the student feels about what happened.
- Praise the student for reporting the incident.
- Ask if there were any other incidents that occurred.
- Ask students what they want to happen next and decide on a positive action to undertake immediately. Not responding with an action discourages students from reporting in the future.
- Tell the student what you will do, for example, report what happened to administrators, speak to and discipline the harasser, and/or inform his or her family.
- When unsure of what to do, set up a second meeting with the student within a day or two. During that time seek advice from others, such as the counselor, principal, vice principal, or site complaint manager, and be sure to talk to the student again.
- Talk to the targeted student about fear of retaliation. Explain the school's policy on retaliation and how it is implemented. Encourage the student to tell you (or another adult) immediately if there are threats, teasing, or other retaliatory behavior by the harasser or by anyone else.
- Do not expect students to handle incidents on their own, especially those of physical behavior such as touching and groping. When the harassment involves physical behavior such as touching and groping, the harassed student should be referred to the counselor, and the principal or vice principal should be notified immediately. The behavior should be reported to the appropriate state and local authorities.
- When the harassment does not involve physical behavior, inform the student what the school can do as well as suggest some actions that she or he might take if they want to do so. Let harassed students decide whether to try to handle it alone or whether they want someone in authority to intervene. (Do not pressure students to handle behaviors on their own unless you are certain they can do so and are willing and eager to do it. In those cases, students need to know that the school will be backing them up, and if the strategy fails, the school will step

in.) If a student decides to try to handle an incident by him- or herself, follow-up is essential to determine if the student's response was successful or if further intervention by the school is needed.

Suggestions for student action include the following:

- Telling the harasser to stop in a very firm way if the student has not already done so. (Telling the harasser to stop sometimes works, but not always.)
  - —I don't want you to say that to me ever again.
  - —I want you to leave me alone.
  - —This is sexual harassment and I want it to stop right now.
  - —I don't think that is funny at all and I don't want you to say things like that to me.
  - —You have two choices. You can keep on doing what you are doing and I will report it to _____ today, or you can stop this right now and walk away and never do it again. It's your choice. Now what do you want to do?
- Having the student rehearse the statement aloud, as well as providing information on how to respond if the harassment continues or the harasser becomes angry, abusive, or threatening, is often helpful.
- Alternatively, the student could write the harasser a letter about the harassment.[8] This technique involves the student writing a specific type of letter to the harasser. Part I of the letter describes what happened. Part II describes how the student feels about it, and Part III, what action the student wants to happen now. The letter is then read aloud to the harasser in a private conversation by an adult authority, such as the teacher, principal, or counselor. The student who wrote the letter may or may not be present, depending on what the student wants. A discussion with the harasser about what happened and possible consequences should follow.

Sample Letter from a Student Who Is Being Harassed

Dear Tyrone,

(Part I)   You are calling me names that I don't like. You called me a "slut" and a "ho" and "a bitch." You stare at my breasts and

make jokes about them. Last week you lied to your friends
and told them that you and I made out. That isn't true and you
know that.

(Part II)   You are making me very angry. I don't like what you are doing. I don't think it is funny at all. It isn't fair and it makes me
feel very bad.

(Part II)   I want you to stop calling me names. I want you to stop staring at my breasts and making jokes about them. I want you to
stop telling lies about me.

Amanda

- Provide access to counseling. Sexual harassment, especially when repeated, can be traumatic. Students may feel angry, depressed, and upset. Both the student and the family should be informed that counseling is available. When needed, the student should be referred directly to the school counselor. It is also important to follow up a week or two later (and again if necessary) to determine whether the student saw the counselor and if any other referrals are necessary.
- If the student mentions thoughts of suicide, report it *immediately* to the principal so that professional help can be obtained quickly. Make sure that the family is also immediately informed.
- Follow the school's policy in reporting the sexually harassing incident to the proper persons. Remember that all incidents of improper touching should be reported under most state laws. When in doubt about whom to report the information to, report it to the principal.
- Keep a dated record of what the student told you and how you responded, as described in appendix A.
- After the school has talked to the harasser, disciplined the student, or taken other actions, inform the harassed student what has been done. A sample letter appears later in this section. (The more serious the incident, the more important it is that the family also be notified about actions taken.) It is helpful at this point to remind the harassed student again that retaliation of any sort is prohibited and to encourage the harassed student to report it if it occurs. Request additional information from the student if needed.

- If either the student or the family is not pleased with the school's response, encourage them to talk to the site complaint manager, the principal, or the sexual harassment administrator. Request additional information from the student or family if needed.
- Monitor the behavior of the harasser and the harassed student closely. Check with the harassed student several times to ensure that the harassment has stopped, that no retaliation from the harasser or other students has taken place, and decide whether any additional action is necessary.

What to Do When Students Ask You Not to Tell Anyone Else

Often students want to confide in an adult but are afraid to "officially" report sexually harassing behavior. Sometimes they will say they can't tell you what happened unless you promise to keep it secret. Here are some ways to respond, although not necessarily in this order.

- Ask the student what she or he is afraid of. Almost always the student will describe a fear of retaliation and/or lack of confidentiality.
- Describe how the district policy specifically prohibits retaliation and responds to it effectively. Include that many times sexually harassing behavior is against the law.
- Describe what the district will do to protect a student and to stop retaliation if it occurs.

> We would talk to the person bothering you and tell him (her) that if they or their friends bother you, they will be in serious trouble and be punished severely. We can put them in another class or another school, or even suspend or expel students who retaliate in any way whatsoever. We tell the students that we will be watching them to see that there is no retaliation. We can also meet with your class and let everyone know that retaliation against anyone who reports sexually harassing behavior would be violating our school and district policy. We watch the person bothering you to make sure that there is no retaliation. If you came and told us that there was any retaliation we would act immediately to stop it.

- Explain the confidentiality policy.

  The only people at school who would know about what happened are those who would need to know, such as your teacher, the vice principal and the principal.

- Explain what happens when someone complains.

  I or someone else can talk to the student who harassed you and often that stops the problem. We can also punish that student. If that doesn't stop the problem, we can do other things as well, such as moving the student to another class or school. We would not allow that person to continue treating you badly.

- Explain why you must tell others in the school about sexually harassing behavior.

  I can see that you are very upset about this and I don't want anyone else to go through what you are going through. Our school takes sexual harassment very seriously and I would have to tell someone else so we can deal with the problem and stop it from happening to you or anyone else. If someone is being treated badly in our school we have to do something about it. So I can't promise not to tell anyone, but I would only tell those people who need to know about the behavior so we can all stop it from happening again.

Generally, when these procedures are followed, the student is relieved that the incident is taken seriously and feels protected. As a result, the student will often agree to share the information.

If the student should decide not to tell you about what happened, the following might be helpful.

- Ask the student to think about it some more and set an appointment time to discuss it further. If the student does not want to set another appointment, encourage her (him) to come back if she or he wants to talk some more or has any other questions (they might be more comfortable with someone else).
- Suggest that the student might talk to the school counselor to help deal with feelings about the incident(s).

- Explain that writing things down often helps people figure out what to do next. Ask the student to write down what has already happened and any new incidents that occur.
- Express your hope that the student will talk with you sometime soon.
- Ask if the student would like some strategies to try to deal with the incident. Do not suggest this if you have any suspicion that the behavior involves sexual abuse, assault, physical threats, or stalking.
- Devise a plan to involve others (such as the teacher, cafeteria staff, bus driver, and aides) to monitor the student's behavior in class and elsewhere to see whether the identity of the harasser(s) can be found and to assess if the student needs any additional help (such as involving the school counselor directly).

What to Do When No One Complains

Sometimes the school has reason to believe that a particular student has engaged in sexual harassment but no one has come forward to complain about the behavior nor is there enough information to be certain about what happened. Here is one way to respond: have an administrator with authority (e.g., a principal or superintendent rather than a counselor) speak to the student believed to be engaging in harassing behavior.

- The student should be told that the school has reason to believe that the student has engaged in sexual harassment and that even though there is no accusation or evidence at this point, the school would like to talk with him or her.
- The administrator should review the alleged behavior and point out that such behavior, *if it occurred*, would be a violation of school policy and *if* the student engaged in such behavior in the future there would be sanctions.
- The school policy on sexual harassment should be reviewed as well as its policy against retaliation, and the student given a copy of the policy.
- The administrator may make suggestions about the student's future behavior and also state that the student's behavior will be

monitored in the future to ensure that there is no sexual harassment or retaliation.

- The administrator should involve appropriate personnel in monitoring the student's behavior.
- The administrator should write a memo to the files about the conversation and follow-up plan.

If the administrator knows which students have been harassed, the administrator may want to inform them that he or she has spoken to the other student, explain what the conversation was, and ask them to inform the school if the harassment continues or if there is any retaliation. The administrator should write a memo to the files about this conversation also.

HOW TO HELP STUDENTS WHO HARASS

Students who engage in harassment do so for a wide range of reasons. Whatever the reason, this behavior needs to be stopped. This can be accomplished in a variety of ways. For some, simply having an adult name and/or describe the behavior and *apply a consequence* will stop the behavior. For those who repeatedly harass other students despite consistent interventions and discipline, additional strategies are necessary. Such persistent harassing behavior can be a symptom of severe emotional problems. Like other sexual harassment it should *not* be brushed off as "boys will be boys" or viewed as "cultural differences."

- Be consistent in intervening and applying discipline for sexual harassment.
- Insist that the harasser apologize orally or in writing to the student who was harassed. The apology should include a description of the behavior.
- Use a "Thinking about Your Behavior" sheet, which asks the student to think about the behavior he or she engaged in by answering questions such as:
  —What is the rule that I broke?
  —What did I do that broke the rule?

—Why did I choose to break the rule?

—Who was bothered when I broke the rule?

—What could I have done instead?

—What should I do in the future?

This can be the basis for a discussion later between the student and teacher. The teacher can then express confidence in the student's ability to make better choices in the future. The information helps teachers (or others) assess the student's perception and understanding of what happened.

- Praise the student when he or she is *not* harassing and is behaving better, such as

    You behaved well in class today. I can tell you are taking your behavior seriously and working hard to change it. I was pleased you are treating other students with respect, as when you helped Alvaro with his assignment.

It is particularly effective to recognize positive appropriate behavior at the first available opportunity after a student has been disciplined or reprimanded for harassing behavior. Praise can take many forms, such as a verbal comment; a written note given to the student; a written note to the family that the student sees and takes home; or an e-mail, regular letter, or phone call to the student and family.

- Seek advice from the principal, the counselor, and other staff for additional ways to help the student.
- Arrange for support for the student such as a psychological evaluation, and counseling. Although counseling is often helpful, it should *never* be used as a sanction or instead of a sanction.
- Use all the techniques used with any student who needs help and guidance in social development.
- Strengthen your relationship with the student. Talk to the student about his or her interests and abilities. This personal adult/student relationship is critical for improved student behavior and attitude change. Praise the student for other activities and achievements to help build self-esteem.
- Provide opportunities for developing leadership capacity so that the student uses new behaviors to receive positive recognition, for

example, tutoring a first-grade student, becoming a crossing guard, joining a Boys and Girls Club.

• Involve the family. Families are generally seriously concerned when their child engages in sexual harassment. Sometimes the family may have difficulty understanding that the school has a mandate to provide a safe environment for all students to be able to learn and develop social skills as well as academic skills. Those families who become knowledgeable about sexual harassment issues are more likely to become personally responsible for their child's behaviors. They need to become an active partner with the school to stop this behavior and to be able to offer opportunities for positive social development for their child. Families also need the support and guidance from the teacher and administration.

When working with the family of a student harasser, it is essential to establish this teacher/family partnership in a caring, supportive environment free of "finger pointing" and "blame" language so that neither of the partners engages in defensive behavior. The attitude and suggestions presented by teachers and administrators to the families should convey that student sexual harassment is serious and has long-term effects for both the harassed student and the student engaged in sexually harassing behavior.

It is in the best interest of the student's development for the family, teacher, and other school personnel to develop a joint plan to help the student. Include new ways to help the student receive positive recognition.

HOW TO HANDLE SEXUAL HARASSMENT COMPLAINTS

The majority of sexual harassment incidents and complaints are handled *in an informal manner*. For example, a student complains to a teacher or other staff member, who then intervenes, and the particular behavior stops. In contrast, a *formal* complaint involves using the specific procedures described in the district's sexual harassment policy.

These regulated formal procedures are less likely to be used with very young students. Formal procedures are more likely to be used when the behavior is persistent or pervasive and/or involves physical behavior.

Obligations for All Complaints

Whether a complaint is informal or formal, the district has the same obligation to do the following:

- Stop the harassment against this student and others.
- Prevent its recurrence. Interventions are described elsewhere in this chapter and may include referral to counseling or change of alleged harasser's seating position, class, or school to minimize contact with the complainant before and/or after the complaint is settled. In most instances, if a student is to be moved, the student who engaged in the harassing behavior should be the one to be moved. Occasionally it may be helpful to change the class or school of the student being harassed when it is requested by the student or family.
- Help the victim deal with any current and lingering effects of sexual harassment.
- Help the harassers deal with the consequences of their behavior and stop harassing others.
- Keep records of what happened.
- Follow up with victims, including ensuring that the harassment has stopped, that no retaliation is occurring, and that no further interventions are needed.

Informal Complaints

The vast majority of sexual harassment complaints are handled informally, in part because students, like adults who are harassed, generally do not want to file formal charges. Their usual immediate goal when harassment first occurs is for the behavior to stop (rather than to punish the offender) and to prevent this behavior in the future. Informal handling is more flexible, with fewer required procedures. For example, informal complaints typically do not require that a complaint be in writing. Simply telling an adult about one or more incidents is enough to trigger a response from the school, as well as the school's learning about the incident(s) from another source.

Incidents are typically resolved more quickly when handled informally than when formal procedures are invoked. Whether the definition of sexual harassment exactly fits the description in the district policy is not as important in informal handling because the aim of the resolution of the incident(s) is *to stop the offending behavior* rather than determine whether the behavior is sexual harassment as defined in the policy and whether the policy was violated.

Informal procedures can usually provide more confidentially for both parties. Many times, informal procedures may not require an investigation, because often the student who harassed admits that he or she engaged in the behavior or it was observed by other students or adults. That is sufficient information for teachers or other staff to then be able to proceed without a formal investigation. When formal charges are filed, the behavior is usually more serious and an investigation is required because more severe consequences are involved. The more serious the harassment, the less likely that informal procedures will (or should) be used.

Teachers and principals are often able to stop harassment by talking to the student who is harassing others and by punishing the student for such behavior. The victim and the district or school have a number of options that they can pursue, as discussed earlier. In some instances, students may wish to handle an incident on their own, with teachers and counselors providing the student with specific advice on what to do. However, staff need to monitor the situation and be ready to intervene if the student is unsuccessful in stopping the behavior or if retaliation occurs.

When the complaint is handled informally, teachers and principals can quickly determine the consequences for the harasser. The more serious responses, such as suspension and expulsion, often require that certain formal procedures be followed. Informal methods are often useful when incidents are disputed and unable to be proved.

Formal Complaints

Formal procedures are used less frequently than informal procedures. When a formal complaint is filed, the aim is to find out if the accused student violated the district's policy, and to respond accordingly. Usually, complaints must be in writing from the harassed student or family for formal procedures to be invoked. These procedures must then follow precisely those described in the written policy. Family members and school personnel (as well as older students) should be able to put a complaint in writing when they want to invoke formal procedures. If students or a family cannot put their complaint in writing or are uneasy about doing so, the site complaint manager or someone else should write the complaint for them and ask them to sign it. *Students should never be forced to put a complaint in writing in order to have the district respond informally or formally. The fact that a complaint is not in writing does not weaken the district's responsibility to deal with the complaint.*

Formal procedures should also be able to be invoked by the school itself without a written complaint from a student or family.

Formal procedures are less flexible, and almost always require an investigation (see appendix B).

It is usually harder to maintain confidentiality when formal procedures are used.

Consequences may be more serious and include expulsion or suspension.

Formal procedures are often used when:

- A harassed student (and/or their family) requests it, because informal procedures have failed or because he or she does not want to use the informal procedures.
- The district or school has not handled the complaint informally to the student's and/or family's satisfaction.
- The district or school files its own charge against a student.
- Criminal laws are involved, such as in sexual assault or sexual abuse.

Formal procedures can be stopped if there is an agreement or resolution to which the school, the harasser, *and* the complainant agree.

After the Informal or Formal Resolution of a Complaint

Write a letter to the students involved. (In the case of younger students a letter might be sent just to their families.) In both informal and formal complaints, it is helpful for a staff member such as the sexual harassment administrator, principal, or complaint manager to summarize separately, orally, and in writing to both students involved. In the case of a formal complaint, the letter would be more detailed, including information about the process.

The letter helps ensure that the students involved understand that the incident in question violated the school's policy, that the school has responded and stopped the behavior, and that the school takes these incidents seriously. It should contain the following, although not necessarily in this order:

- A description of the incident, including date and place
- The name of the person to whom the incident was reported
- A statement that the school's policy prohibits sexual harassment
- An acknowledgment that the policy was violated
- Notification that the harasser was told about the policy concerning retaliation
- A description of how the incident was resolved, including punishment and letter of apology, if any
- Reiteration of the prohibition against retaliation (describing examples, including retaliation by friends of the accused student)
- A description of others who know about the incident and what happened subsequently, if relevant
- Information that the incident was reported to both students' families (It may not be necessary to report some minor incidents to families.)
- Thanks to the victim for reporting the incident, if applicable
- Responsibility of the teacher and/or other staff members in the future, if applicable
- An offer of continued help if problems continue or new ones arise, including the names of at least two people who can be contacted for help
- An opportunity for the student or family to correct the letter if it is incorrect or if he or she is not satisfied with what happened

SAMPLE LETTERS OF RESOLUTION

Below are examples of letters of resolution to the target of the harassment, to the harassing student, and to the family of each student. The type of information needed is indicated on the left, with suggested text on the right.

Letter to a Target of Harassment

Dear Maria,

Date of incident(s)

Last Tuesday [date] you told me that Jack (last name) had been

Description of incident(s)
Name of person it was reported to

calling you names such as "slut," "bitch," and "whore" in your classroom and in the cafeteria, and that it makes you feel very

Acknowledgment that the behavior violated the policy

uncomfortable and angry. As I explained to you such behavior violates our school district's pol-

Policy summary given to student

icy against sexual harassment. I gave you a summary of our policy. This letter summarizes what has happened since then.

How the incident was handled
Plan of action

You and I discussed what we could do to stop Jack's behavior. You decided that you wanted me to talk to him about his behavior and tell him to stop. I told you I would speak with Jack as soon as possible.

Implementation of plan of action

On Thursday [date] I had a long talk with Jack about his behavior, and told him that his behavior was a violation of our district's sexual harassment policy and that this behavior had to stop immediately. If not, there

Written letter of apology reviewed by school personnel before being given to harassed student

Information about the policy against retaliation given to both students involved

Examples of retaliation

Written statement from harasser promising to follow the school's policy and not engage in the behavior anymore

Description of punishment

Notification that the punishment will increase if the behavior is repeated or if there is any retaliation.

Encouraging the student to report any further problems

Responsibility of the teacher and other staff

will be punishment. He promised me that he would stop at once.

Jack agreed to write you a letter of apology in which he promised you he would not call you names anymore. He gave me his written apology to read, and then I gave it to you on Friday [date] when I told you about my conversation with him.

When I gave you his letter, I also told you that I told Jack that he would be suspended or even expelled if he harassed you again or retaliated against you in any way, such as getting his friends to threaten, tease, or bother you. That would also be a violation of our policy.

I also had him write a letter to me showing that he knew that calling names was against our policy, and that he promised not to do so any more. He will also be given a Saturday morning detention next week. If he behaves badly again, the punishment will be more severe.

If Jack's behavior does not stop or if he or his friends bother you in any way, please let me or Ms. Smith [principal] know immediately, and we will do whatever needs to be done to stop that from happening again.

I also told your teacher, Ms. Fumati, and Ms. Wong, the cafeteria

Who else knows about this

monitor, about what happened and they will try to keep an eye on you and on Jack's behavior.

Making sure the letter is accurate

If this letter is not accurate or if you are not comfortable with how we have dealt with Jack, or if anything is bothering you, or if you have any questions, or if anyone

Giving the student two options for seeking additional help if needed

teases or taunts you because you complained about Jack's behavior, please tell me or Ms. Smith at once so we can help solve the problem.

Who else is getting a copy of the letter

I am sending a copy of this letter to your family as we discussed earlier. I am sending a similar letter to Jack and a copy will be sent to his family.

Praise for the student for reporting the incident

I want to thank you for coming in to tell me about Jack's behavior. I know that was hard for you to do but I am glad that you did because sometimes the school doesn't know when these behaviors exist and we

Reiteration of the school's commitment to end sexual harassment

don't want these kinds of behaviors to occur in our school. You are a good citizen of our school.
Sincerely,
Karen Green, Vice Principal

Letter to the Student Who Harassed

Dear Jack,
This letter summarizes our conversation on Thursday [date].

Date of meeting with student

As you know I called you into my office, to tell you that Maria Hall had complained to me that

Description of incident(s)

you were calling her names such as "slut," "bitch," and "whore" in your classroom and in the cafeteria. We do not allow this kind of hurtful behavior in our school.

Description of the behavior as hurtful

I reminded you that this behavior violates our school policy on sexual harassment and gave you a summary of our policy. You said you didn't know the behavior could get you in trouble.

Acknowledgment that the behavior violated the policy

Policy summary given to student

I asked you to write a letter of apology to Maria, which you did and which I gave to her today.

How the incident was handled

I also asked you to write a letter to me, stating that you understand the policy and that you promised not to call anyone names like that again. You also promised in the letter not to bother or threaten Maria, or encourage your friends to bother or threaten her because she reported your behavior to the school.

Request for a letter of apology

Letter of apology given by staff to student who was harassed

Letter from harassing student promising to stop the behavior

Promise not to retaliate

Examples of retaliation

I have spoken to your teacher, Ms. Fumati, and Ms. Wong, the cafeteria monitor, about what has happened and they will be monitoring your behavior to see that this does not happen again.

Plans to watch the student's behavior

Because this was the first time you were reported doing this, the punishment will be one Saturday morning detention, on [date]. If you engage in this or any other

Description and date of punishment

Notification that punishment will increase if behavior is repeated or if there is retaliation

sexual harassment, or if there is any retaliation, the punishment will be more severe and could even include expulsion.

Who else is getting a copy of this letter

As we discussed earlier I am sending a copy of this letter, as well as the letter you wrote to me promising not to behave this way, to your family and to Maria and her family.

Making sure the letter is accurate

If this letter is inaccurate or if you are not satisfied with how we have dealt with this incident, please let me know. I hope that you will come to me or other

Offer of help if needed

people in our school if you have any more problems.

Expectations for the future

I know you want to behave well and that you will keep your promise.
Sincerely,
Karen Green, Vice Principal

Letter of Resolution to Family of a Harassed Student

Description of incident(s)

Dear Mr. and Mrs. Thomas:
I want to inform you what has happened with your son Jason's complaint. He reported that another student, Mitchell Dunne, called him "gay" and other similar names on several occasions

Date of Incident(s)

during the past two weeks.
Jason told this to Ms. Hammid,

Name of person it was reported to

his English teacher, on [date]. Ms. Hammid told Jason to come to my office.

Family notification

Statement that behavior violates the policy

Policy summary given to harassed student

How incident was handled

Plan of action

Implementation of plan of action

Description of punishment

Notification that punishment will increase if the behavior is repeated or if there is retaliation

Information about retaliation policy given to accused student

After he told me what Mitchell said, I contacted both you and Mitchell's parents about the incident on the same day I informed Mitchell, his parents, and you that such behavior violates our sexual harassment policy. I also gave Jason a summary of the policy

After speaking with Jason about what happened, I met with Mitchell on [date] and informed him of the serious nature of his behavior. Mitchell did not deny that he had called Jason these names. I explained that such behavior violates our sexual harassment policy and emphasized how such behavior affects other people. I gave Mitchell a summary of our policy. As a result of our discussion, Mitchell agreed to write a letter of apology to Jason. In the letter, Mitchell promised not to engage in such behavior again. After approving the letter of apology, I gave it to Jason on [date] and discussed the contents with him.

Mitchell was suspended for only one day because this was the first time he was accused of such behavior. He was informed that if such behavior occurred again, he could face a longer suspension or even expulsion.

I informed Mitchell that retaliation against Jason by him or his

Letter from harassing student
promising to stop behavior

Promise not to retaliate

Examples of retaliation

Supportive measures

Follow-up monitoring

friends was also a violation of our policy.

I also asked Mitchell to write a letter to me stating that he understood the policy and promised not to call Jason or anyone else names like that again, and to promise not to bother or threaten Jason, or encourage his friends to bother or threaten him because he reported Mitchell's behavior.

When I met with Jason to give him Mitchell's letter of apology, I reminded him that the policy also prohibits any form of retaliation against him by Mitchell or anyone else. I asked him to let me know immediately if he experiences any further harassment or retaliation from anyone. I informed him that I will intervene to stop such behavior. Jason found the letter of apology acceptable and therefore does not plan any further action against Mitchell. I will check with both Jason and Mitchell next week, and again in about a month to see whether the harassment has stopped and whether any further action is necessary.

I have talked with both Mitchell's and Jason's teachers about these incidents and have reminded them to inform me if they learn of any sexually harassing behavior by any student.

Follow-up with teachers and principals	*The principal, Ms. Kyla Moran, has sent a letter to all teachers reminding them that such behavior violates our district policy on sexual harassment and that such behavior must be reported to the school.*
Additional preventive measure	*Next month's training session for students concerning sexual harassment will include additional materials on harassment based on sexual orientation.*
	I assume that this matter is now closed and has been resolved satisfactorily. If you or Jason have
Encouragement to contact school again if needed	*any questions, please let me know or contact the guidance counselor.*
	Sincerely,
	Sara Gold, Vice Principal

Letter to Family of Student Who Harassed

	Dear Mr. and Mrs. Dunn:
	I want to inform you what has happened with the complaint against your son, Mitchell. Jason Thomas reported that Mitchell
Description of incident(s)	*called him "gay" and other names on several occasions dur-*
Date of incident(s)	*ing the past two weeks.*
	Jason told this to Ms. Hammid, his English teacher, on [date]. Ms. Hammid told Jason to come to my office. After he told me what Mitchell said, I contacted you as well as Jason's parents on

Family notification statement that behavior violated the policy

How incident was handled

Policy summary given to accused student

Plan of action

Implementation of plan of action

Description of punishment

Notification that punishment will increase if the behavior is repeated or if there is retaliation

Information about retaliation policy given to accused student

Letter from harassing student promising to stop the behavior

the same day about the incidents. I informed you that such behavior violates our sexual harassment policy.

After speaking with you about what happened, I met with Mitchell on [date] and informed him of the serious nature of his behavior. Mitchell did not deny that he had called Jason these names. I explained that such behavior violates our sexual harassment policy and emphasized how such behavior affects other people. I gave him a summary of our policy.

As a result of our discussion, Mitchell agreed to write a letter of apology to Jason. In the letter, Mitchell promised not to engage in such behavior again. After approving the letter of apology, I gave it to Jason on [date] and discussed the contents with him.

Mitchell was suspended for only one day because this was the first time he was accused of such behavior. He was informed that if such behavior occurred again, he could face a longer suspension or even expulsion.

I informed Mitchell that retaliation against Jason by him or his friends was also a violation of our policy.

I also asked Mitchell to write a letter to me stating that he understood

Promise not to retaliate

Examples of retaliation

Follow-up monitoring

Follow-up with teachers and principal

the policy and promised not to call Jason or anyone else names like that again, and to promise not to bother or threaten Jason, or encourage his friends to bother or threaten him because he reported Jason's behavior.

When I met with Jason to give him Mitchell's letter of apology, I reminded him that the policy also prohibits any form of retaliation against him by Mitchell or anyone else. I asked him to let me know immediately if he experiences any further harassment or retaliation from anyone. I informed him that I will intervene to stop such behavior. Jason found the letter of apology acceptable and therefore does not plan any further action against Mitchell. I will check with both Jason and Mitchell next week, and again in about a month to see whether the harassment has stopped and whether any further action is necessary.

I have talked with both Mitchell's and Jason's teachers about these incidents and have reminded them to inform me if they learn of any sexually harassing behavior by any student. The principal, Ms. Kyla Moran, has sent a letter to all teachers reminding them that such behavior violates our district policy on sexual harassment and that such behavior must

Making sure there are no unre-
solved issues

Encouragement to contact school
again if needed.

*be reported to the school. Next
month's training session for students concerning sexual harassment will include additional materials on harassment based on
sexual orientation or perceived
sexual orientation.*

*I assume that this matter is now
closed and has been resolved sat-
isfactorily. If you or Mitchell have
any questions, please let me know
or contact the guidance counselor.
Sincerely,
Sara Gold, Vice Principal*

After the letters of resolution are sent:

- Write a final memo to the files, describing the incident and how it
  was handled. Include copies of all materials, including the letters
  sent to students and their families.
- Follow up with each student about a week after the letter has been
  sent, and again about a month later or earlier if needed, to ensure
  that there is no further harassment or retaliation and to ascertain
  whether any follow-up action, such as counseling, is needed for either student. Checking with each student about the incident em-
  phasizes the seriousness of the behavior and the school's commitment to not tolerate such behavior. Put the follow-up dates on your
  calendar or other reminder.
- Include a memo in the file about results and date(s) of the follow-up.

HOW TO DEAL WITH VIDEO AND COMPUTER HARASSMENT

In some schools students have used school computers to send sexually
harassing messages to other students or insert sexually explicit messages or materials into the school computers. Others have used home
computers and websites to do the same. Within minutes, sexually ha-

rassing materials, sexual slurs, and other demeaning comments can be disseminated to hundreds or even thousands of others via e-mail or websites.

Two male seniors at Horace Greeley High School in Chappaqua, New York, were arrested for posting a website that listed names, phone numbers, and what were said to be the sexual exploits of dozens of female classmates. The site also commented on students' appearance, eating habits, and other personal information. The boys were charged with aggravated harassment.[9]

Similarly, at several selective private schools in New York City students went to a website to vote for the students they considered to be the most promiscuous. They voted on about 150 names, with girls' names outnumbering boys' by 3 to 1. The site was shut down after parents and students complained.[10]

A California sophomore girl was named "ugliest girl" in her class on a website, and then "ugliest girl" in her school. After a rumor circulated that there was a video showing her having sex with several boys at a party, students began calling her "slut" and "whore." Her mother, dissatisfied with the school's response to her complaints, filed a lawsuit against the school district. The student also transferred to an out-of-district high school.[11]

Videos have also been used in ways that violate sexual harassment policies.

A boy at Baltimore's prestigious St. Paul's private school secretly videotaped himself having sex with a fifteen-year-old girl and then played the tape on two occasions for his lacrosse teammates.

When the school learned of it, the rest of the top-ranked lacrosse team's season was canceled, thirty students who saw the tape were suspended, and the boy who made the tape expelled.[12]

Although some schools believe that nothing can be done about sexually harassing e-mails as long as they are not appearing on school computers, other schools include sexually harassing materials about students appearing in private e-mails and websites as violations of their policy. Many of the suggestions given in chapter 5 are applicable to computer harassment issues. Schools can also do the following:

- Ensure that there is a clear policy that videos, websites, and e-mail messages, including instant messaging, on both home and school computers, which have the effect of sexually harassing one or more students are considered violations of the sexual harassment policy and will be handled in the same manner as other violations of that policy.
- Be sure students understand that the school is seriously concerned about computer harassment originating from home computers because such harassment can affect a student's performance and behavior.
- Include information about computer harassment in all training programs for administrators, teachers, staff, and students about sexual harassment.
- Develop written materials about computer harassment to disseminate to administrators, teachers, staff, and students. Ensure that students and staff know that computer harassment is not protected by the constitutional right to free speech. (See chapter 2.) Students might be enlisted to develop specific materials for students use in describing the policy.
- Ensure that computer personnel have specific training about their obligation to follow sexual harassment policy and procedures when harassment occurs on home or school computers.
- Provide students with examples of computer harassment.
- Include loss of school computer time or computer use as one of the sanctions when home or school computers have been used to sexually harass students.
- Include information about computer harassment on bulletin boards displaying information about computers.
- Require students using school computers to sign a pledge stating that they have read the policy and will abide by it, and promising to refrain from using school and home computers to sexually harass other students. The pledge should include information that student families will be informed should the policy be violated. Such a pledge is best preceded by a discussion about sexual ha-

rassment. A committee of students and staff could help draft the pledge.

- Include the prohibition against computer sexual harassment among the general rules for computer use.
- Post information about computer sexual harassment in computer labs and near classroom computers. Develop posters to do so.
- Remind students that the policy covers website space allocated to students to create their own website. Designate someone to review and approve the website content before the material is posted.
- If knowledge of harassing incidents is well-known to many students, ensure that the response includes notifying the student body how the incident was handled and what punishment was invoked.
- Ensure that targets of computer sexual harassment are informed as to how the incident was resolved and that counseling is available if needed or wanted.
- Send families a separate notification informing them about the policy prohibiting students from using home or school computers for sexually harassing other students. Provide examples and describe the harm that sexual harassment can cause. Develop a list of questions that they can use to discuss the policy and issues with their child. A committee of students could help develop such a list.

The Massachusetts Institute of Technology has developed a set of procedures to deal with computer harassment on its computer networks. The Stopit program is based on a simple proposition: that most offenders, given the opportunity to stop uncivil behavior without having to admit guilt, will do so. Although the program was developed for campus use, it can also be used with middle and high school students when students have their own e-mail addresses, passwords, and websites on school computers.

When a student reports sexually harassing computer content, a senior person responds quickly. (In a school, this might be the vice-principal.) A carefully structured standard note is sent to alleged perpetrators: "Someone using your account did [whatever the offense is]." The note then explains why the behavior is offensive or violates MIT's harassment policy, rules of use, or other guidelines, and continues: "Account holders are responsible for the use of their accounts. If you are unaware that your account was being used this way, it may have been compromised." The student is then given detailed instructions on how to change their password.

The note concludes, "If you were aware that your account was being used to [whatever it was], then we trust you will take steps to ensure that this does not happen again."

The results have been highly effective. Many recipients report that their accounts have been compromised and have changed their password (even though it is clear from eyewitnesses or other evidence that they personally were the offenders). Even more important, there is virtually no repetition of the offending or harassing behavior. Even though the recipient concedes no guilt and there is no punishment, the behavior stops.[13]

NOTES

1. L. Phillips, *The Girl's Report: What We Know and Need to Know about Growing Up Female* (The National Council for Research on Women, 1998), p. 49.

2. Middle school girl, cited in J. Shakeshaft, C. Mandel, L. Johnson, Y. M. Sawyer, M. A. Hergenrother, and E. Barber, "Boys Call Me Cow," *Educational Leadership*, October 1997.

3. B. Chase, president, National Education Association, March 25, 2001.

4. L. Walls, "Bullying and Sexual Harassment in Schools," n.d. Retrieved June 26, 2004, from www.cfchildren.org/article_walls1.stml.

5. See *Davis v. Monroe Board of Education* 119 S.Ct. 1661 (1999).

6. "Boy Suspended after Prank," *Educators Guide to Controlling Sexual Harassment,* Monthly Bulletin, April 1999, p. 8.

7. Nan Stein, of the Wellesley College Center for Research on Women, "When 'Good Girls' Get a Bad Rep," *Washington Post*, August 24, 1999.

8. The letter technique was originally developed by Dr. Mary Rowe, Massachusetts Institute of Technology.

9. Two seniors in a small-town New York high school ran a website where they posted alleged sexual information about forty girls. The boys were charged with second-degree aggravated assault. *Associated Press*, June 6, 2001.

10. "Latest High School Sex Gossip Is Now Scrawled on Website Walls," *New York Times*, May 6, 2001.

11. "Student Sues School District after Named on Internet," *Educators' Guide to Controlling Sexual Harassment,* Monthly Bulletin, February 2002.

12. "Dangerous Games, a Sex Video Broke the Rules, but for the Kids the Rules Have Changed," *Washington Post*, April 15, 2001.

13. The idea for the Stopit program emerged from a collaboration among Mary P. Rowe, special assistant to the president, and a group of information systems managed led by Gregory A. Jackson, director of academic computing; Daniel M. Weir, director of computing support services; and Cecelia R. D'Olivera, director of distributed computing network services. For further information, see Jackson's article, "Promoting Civility on the Academic Network: Crime and Punishment, or the Golden Rule?" in *Educational Record*, 75:3, Summer 1994.

CHAPTER 7

How Teachers Can Create a Positive Environment in the Classroom

One of the strongest strategies for preventing sexual harassment is creating a positive school and classroom climate in which students respect each other and which facilitates learning and social development.

In this section you will find specific techniques to incorporate into the general classroom curriculum:

Teacher Strategies for Classroom Use
How to Conduct a Student Discussion about Sexual Harassment
Additional Strategies for Teachers

Some strategies may be more appropriate for the elementary, middle, or high schools.

TEACHER STRATEGIES FOR CLASSROOM USE

- Promote activities that encourage friendship, cooperation, and sharing in order to build acceptance among students. When students know and like each other they are less likely to harass. They are also more likely to intervene when they see others being harassed.
- Establish small groups of students to work together in cooperative units.
- Utilize team projects in subject areas such as science and sports, and with computers.
- Promote activities in which boys and girls, including different racial and ethnic groups, participate together to complete an academic or

school project. Encourage friendships between boys and girls. Establishing a team of boys opposing a team of girls as in physical education or spelling contests creates adversarial relationships between girls and boys. It also violates Title IX, which prohibits schools from discriminating on the basis of sex.

- Incorporate issues of sexism, racism, and homophobia in the curriculum.
- Recognize and reward students for both verbal and nonverbal positive behaviors, for example, when they help each other and exhibit caring and cooperative behaviors ("catch them at being good"). Teachers may present students with a preprinted card describing the type of behavior that is being rewarded, such as "helping someone" or "stopping someone from doing something wrong."

> Alana, I saw you help Omar pick up his books and papers when he dropped them.

> Jared, when you told Max and Steve to "Cool it" on the stairs, it stopped the possibility of a fight. Good work.

- Encourage students to tell the teacher when they notice other students' positive behavior.
- Develop a class pledge about respecting other students. Have each student sign it, and post it for easy and frequent viewing.
- Develop with students a list of what kinds of behaviors are not allowed as well as class rules about positive relationships. If general descriptions are used, such as "making someone feel bad," they should be followed by specific examples, such as "calling people names." Post them in the classroom.
- Develop with students a list of "hurtful words." Post them in the classroom. Discuss how students feel when these words are aimed at them.
- Designate your classroom as a "Sexual Harassment-Free Zone."
- Teach students how to observe sexually harassing behaviors. Develop a class assignment for recording sexual gestures, remarks, and other behaviors that they observe throughout the school.
- Discuss with students the school's Student Bill of Rights and post it in the classroom.

- Provide resources about sexual harassment, including articles, books, and videos appropriate for students. Have them available in the school library or in the classroom.
- Invite the principal to meet with the class. Have the students describe what actions they are taking to prevent and deal with sexual harassment.
- Encourage a press release about the class's activities to be sent to the school and local papers. Check with the principal for permission.

HOW TO CONDUCT A STUDENT DISCUSSION ABOUT SEXUAL HARASSMENT

When students are educated in recognizing hurtful behavior, they are probably more apt to step in and stop it.[1]

The sexual harassment curriculum is really doing the school some good. One of the harassers who has always been harassing any girls at all has stopped. [He] has stopped goosing and touching girls. I never thought I'd see the day—he no longer pinches girls and rubs up against them in the hall. People are more conscious about what they say and how they use words like gay, faggot, and lesbian. They realize that some people could really be offended by it. (eighth-grade male student)[2]

Before undertaking a classroom discussion, the teacher should be familiar with sexual harassment issues, the district's policy, and the consequences of sexual harassment.

In conducting such discussions it is helpful to tell the students that there will be guidelines for the sexual harassment discussion. A handout describing the guidelines should be provided to each student. Ask a student to read the guidelines aloud and ask if there are any questions. Ask the students to sign the agreement to follow the guidelines. The signed agreements should be returned to the teacher.

Sample Guidelines for Student Discussion about Sexual Harassment

To show respect for myself and others I agree:

1. To be as honest as possible
2. To listen carefully without interrupting other people

3. To speak one at a time so everyone can be heard
4. To not put anyone down or call anyone names even when we disagree
5. To use respectful language in our discussions
6. To let others know when I feel disrespected or put down by something said by another student
7. To not mention the names of anyone when I describe incidents I know about
8. To not hit anyone

Signed _____   _____
              Name of Student   Name of Teacher

(These guidelines are adapted from the "Roads to Respect Program," which is part of the "Witherbee Program" at the Rape Treatment Center of Santa Monica–UCLA Medical Center, Santa Monica, California.)

Questions for Student Discussions

Depending on the time allocated for discussion, the questions may need to be discussed in more than one session.

Ask students to think about times that they were excluded or treated differently by other students, such as the following:

- Were you ever not allowed to play a game or be friends with someone?
- Were you ever ridiculed because of the way you looked or behaved?
- Have you ever felt left out or put down, taunted or teased, because you didn't measure up to your friends' or peers' ideal of how a boy or girl should look or act?
- How do you think students feel if they are treated this way?
- Do you know what sexual harassment is? Ask for examples. (Remind them not to mention anyone's name.)
- How do you think the students who were sexually harassed felt?
- How would you feel if this happened to your friend?
- Why do you think some students sexually harass other students?

The following questions can be used to help students develop strategies for responding when they see one student harassing another, how to support a student who intervenes, and what to do if they themselves are harassed. Having students say these responses aloud in unison and in a strong voice as well as demonstrating the strategies in a role play is helpful. Students generally enjoy learning how to stand up for themselves and how to help others do so.

- What can students do to help someone who is being harassed?
- What can you do or say?
  - Provide examples when needed such as saying: "That's sexual harassment and it's wrong! Mary doesn't like it, and I don't like it! I want you to stop it right now!" Naming the behavior as "sexual harassment" is a useful strategy.
  - A similar statement can be used by someone who is actually being harassed: "You're sexually harassing me. I don't like it and nobody else likes it either. You need to stop this right now!"
- How can you support a fellow student who is trying to stop sexual harassment?
  - One example: "You heard what Michael said. Don't do that again!"

Encourage students to report sexual harassing behaviors with discussion about the following:

- Why students should report sexual harassment.
- The school's policy and the consequences for sexually harassing another student. (Hand out summaries of the school policy if available.)
- What happens when an incident is reported.
- How complaints are handled, including informal ways of dealing with it.
- What the follow-up is after a complaint (to show that the complaint was dealt with effectively).
- Why it is important to tell an adult when a student is harassed, threatened, or intimidated in any manner.
- The differences between reporting to protect another student or one's self, and "snitching" or "ratting" or "tattling" to get someone in trouble.

- Whom to tell if you are harassed or see someone being harassed. Be sure everyone knows several adults whom they can tell, such as the teacher, principal, vice principal, site complaint manager, sexual harassment coordinator, and counselor. Encourage students to also tell their families.

Inform the students that the school will not tolerate any retaliation against anyone reporting an incident. Retaliation includes harmful actions to someone who complained about sexual harassment or assisted in the complaint process in any way. Give examples of retaliation and the kinds of behaviors that the school will not tolerate, such as:

Examples of Retaliation

- Continued or worsening sexual harassment
- Physical harm, such as hitting, shoving, pushing
- Teasing or taunting by students involved in the complaint or their friends
- Making or carrying out any threats whatsoever, such as threatening to "get even" or to harm the student, his or her friends, family, pets, or property
- Blaming the victim for the harassment itself and for its consequences
- Destruction of or stealing a student's property, such as throwing a backpack into a puddle
- Intimidating behavior of any kind, such as standing very close to the student(s) involved in the complaint, staring, muttering hostile comments
- Making obnoxious noises such as sucking sounds or deliberate belching
- Sending negative notes or e-mails or making annoying phone calls
- Telling other students negative information or rumors about the student(s) involved in the complaint
- Following or stalking a person
- Getting other students to do any of the above

Describe what steps the school will take to protect students against retaliation. Before ending the discussion:

- Allow time for additional questions.
- Briefly summarize the main points of the discussion.
- Encourage students to suggest additional follow-up activities.
- Let students know that you and the counselor are available privately to answer additional questions about sexual harassment.
- Announce the date for the next discussion and what the topics will be.

ADDITIONAL STRATEGIES FOR TEACHERS

Conduct a ten-minute discussion periodically about how students relate to each other. Encourage students to discuss their feelings. Although teacher time is limited, time spent on talking about relationships and feelings may well mean less time spent in disciplining students and more time for the curriculum.

Use the curriculum to reinforce the theme of eliminating sexual harassment. For example, in Language Arts have students keep a journal about any sexually harassing behaviors they observe. Use library books focusing on these issues. In Social Studies have students use newspapers and magazines to discuss events relating to sexual harassment.

Encourage students to form or join a school leadership group to educate students about sexual harassment.

NOTES

1. L. Walls, "Bullying and Sexual Harassment in Schools," n.d. Retrieved June 26, 2004, from www.cfchildren.org/article_walls1.stml.

2. N. Stein, "Sexual Harassment in School: The Public Performance of Gendered Violence," *Harvard Educational Review* 65, 2 (Summer 1995).

CHAPTER 8

How to Engage Families and Communities in School Sexual Harassment Issues

This chapter contains strategies to work directly with families and how to reach out and involve the community:

How to Involve Families
How to Involve the Community

HOW TO INVOLVE FAMILIES

Involving families in sexual harassment issues can make a major difference in how their children behave at school. Here are some things schools can do to help families become involved in these issues:

- Send home materials describing what sexual harassment behavior is, the school's policy on student-to-student sexual harassment, and the consequences of such behaviors. Ask for the family's support. A sample letter to family members appears later in this chapter.
- Include school sexual harassment as one of the topics covered on Open School Night, at conferences, and at meetings. Talk to family members about the school's mission to provide a school environment safe for all students to learn and to develop. This includes the elimination of sexual harassment in the school.
- Enlist the support of Parent-Teacher Associations in the dissemination of materials and the inclusion of programs about sexual harassment. Such programs can include a talk from the district office

or by the principal on the impact of sexual harassment on a student's learning ability and social and emotional development, the school policy, federal and state laws and regulations, and what the school is presently doing to prevent sexual harassment.

- Include materials about sexual harassment in packets of information given to families of new and transfer students.
- Send home materials providing suggestions on how family members can talk to their children about sexual harassment. "How Families Can Discuss Sexual Harassment with Their Child" appears later in this chapter.
- Send home a letter describing what the school is doing to reduce hurtful name-calling and other sexually harassing activities. Continue to send other related materials, articles, and information about school activities concerning sexual harassment to families from time to time.
- Enlist family volunteers to provide added supervision in places where student-to-student sexual harassment often occurs, such as hallways, cafeteria, schoolyard, school buses, etc. Some schools have installed video cameras to monitor such areas. (One district, lacking money to install video cameras on all of its school buses, installed dummy cameras on some, and real cameras on the remaining buses. Although students know that some of the cameras are not real, they cannot tell which are the real cameras. Behavior on the buses improved.)
- Provide training to family volunteers on how they are to respond when they observe student-to-student sexual harassment and how to report such incidents.
- Meet periodically with family volunteers to discuss their observations in school. They often can provide important information about what is happening in various parts of the school, such as the cafeteria, schoolyard, and buses.
- Inform families when their child is involved in a sexual harassment incident. Tell the family what they need to do next. Follow up with family members and keep them informed about what the school is doing in response to the incident. Encourage them to work with the school to develop a plan for their child. When seri-

ous incidents frequently occur, also inform the families of students who were present when the harassment occurred.

- Encourage families to inform the school if they believe their child is being sexually harassed. Some families are reluctant to report such behaviors because they may be afraid it will go on the student's record; they may not know what is the best way to deal with it; they are unfamiliar with how the school will respond; and they may fear retaliation for their child if the behavior is reported.

Sample Letter to Families about Sexual Harassment

Dear Family [Family includes all persons caring for students—parents, grandparents, foster parents, child caseworkers, etc.]:

Our school has a strong commitment to create a positive learning environment where all our students can feel safe and secure and ready to learn and grow.

This learning environment includes eliminating any form of student-to-student sexual harassment, which often presents a serious barrier to learning and social development. Many students are exploring their sexuality and some are unsure how to behave. Others may be imitating behaviors they have seen on television or in movies or imitating their peers who are harassing. Some are deliberately trying to intimidate fellow students. They may need to feel "powerful" and they incorrectly believe that sexually harassing someone makes them feel stronger and better than their victims. Whatever the reason, it is dangerous behavior to all who are involved.

Sexual harassment is any form of sexual behavior that makes students feel unsafe and unprotected so that they are unable to focus on learning, studying, achieving, or participating in school activities. It is often a form of bullying, where one or more students intimidate another student by using sexuality as a weapon. The unwelcome behavior can be verbal, such as sexual name-calling, or can be physical, such as unwanted touching.

Sexual harassment occurs between boys and girls and between students of the same gender. Sometimes it involves a group of students harassing others. It also includes harassment of lesbian and gay students or those students assumed to be so.

Our school has moral, legal, and educational obligations to prevent and stop all of these behaviors. If your child has been the victim of harassment, please contact Ms. Green, the principal, or your child's teacher as soon as possible so we can protect your child and others by stopping and punishing such behaviors. Our school is working to develop students who respect each other, cooperate and work together, and use positive behaviors to achieve academically and to develop socially.

Your child needs your support to develop positive behaviors. Find time, perhaps at meals, to talk to your child about this kind of negative behavior.

On [date, time and place] you are invited to join other families to discuss sexual harassment and how best to prevent it from happening. Your child needs your support to become an achieving student and a caring citizen. We will share ideas and welcome your thoughts.

We look forward to meeting you.

(Signed by principal or vice principal)

_____ *Yes, I will attend this important meeting on student sexual harassment on* [date] *at* [time] *in Room* _____

Name _____

Family member of : _____

                    Student's name

Sample Agenda for Sexual Harassment Meeting with Families

Meeting with families helps them learn about student harassment so that they will be supportive of the school's activities. An agenda for such a meeting should include the following:

- Description and examples of sexually harassing behavior
- Moral, legal, educational, social, and emotional implications of peer harassment for students
- The district's strong commitment to preventing and responding to sexual harassment
- Programs the school is developing or utilizing to prevent student-to-student sexual harassment
- What to do if their child reports sexually harassing behaviors to them

- Where to obtain additional information, including a name and phone number, and where to report sexual harassment problems, anonymously if necessary
- Development of a Family Sexual Harassment Study Group

Suggested handouts:

- Copy of policy and/or an easy-to-understand summary (and where to obtain a complete copy)
- A list of examples of sexual harassment
- How sexual harassment affects students
- How to respond when your child tells you that he or she has been harassed (a sample script is helpful)
- Whom to contact for additional information
- A list of resources available in the school and/or the district and their location

How Families Can Discuss Sexual Harassment with Their Child

[Note: These suggestions can be sent to families as an enclosure in a letter about peer harassment, or incorporated into the letter itself.]

- Use an informal setting (in the car, at the mall, while eating together at home or elsewhere, etc.) as an opportunity to talk about sexual harassment. (If using the car, do not turn on the radio.) This is a good time to talk about a news item or article you read about sexual harassment. Discuss what it means and why it is important.
- Ask your child about what happens at school, rather than if he or she has been sexually harassed or harassed anyone else. (Many children do not know the term *sexual harassment* or may not be ready to talk to their family about their own experiences.)
  - —Talk about when you were in school and "there was a lot of teasing."
  - —Ask what kind of teasing occurs in their school.
  - —Ask what happens when these behaviors occur.

— Ask how your child thinks the student being teased or harassed feels.

- Share your own experiences about sexual harassment, whether as a victim at school or at work or as someone who observed it happening to others.
- Encourage your child to be aware of sexual harassment in school. Suggest that he or she keep a journal and act as a journalist. Have the child note what happened, who was harassed, who did the harassing, where it occurred, who was present, and whether anyone intervened. Set a time to discuss the findings.
- View TV programs with your child to see how sexual harassment is handled in sitcoms, which often portray sexual harassment as something humorous and not as something that is hurtful.
  — Does the program make sexual harassment look like a good joke? Is it a joke?
  — How does your child think the person being sexually harassed feels?
  — Would a person in real life feel that way?
  — Would your child like to be treated that way?
- Talk about how this kind of behavior often continues into later life, at the workplace, recreation areas, and family life, and the importance of establishing positive behaviors now in school.
- Discuss sexual harassment with your child periodically. Discussion is not a one-time event. The issue is important and needs to be talked about. TV shows as well as newspapers and magazine articles are good starting points.

HOW TO INVOLVE THE COMMUNITY

Communities play an important role in supporting schools; therefore, it is important for the community at large to become aware of the issue of sexual harassment occurring in schools and in the community. Additionally, student-to-student sexual harassment may also occur in community-supported activities such as after-school sports and clubs. The district and individual schools can take an active role in developing community awareness, support, and activities.

How the District and Individual Schools Can Increase Community Awareness and Develop Activities Concerning Sexual Harassment

- Establish a community committee to begin a Sexual Harassment Awareness Campaign. The committee should include representatives from youth-oriented community programs, family members of local students, and youth members.
- Support outreach to community members such as churches and synagogues, Y's, Boys and Girls Clubs, health clinics, and businesses. Invite representatives to attend a meeting and enlist their commitment that neither verbal nor physical sexual harassment will be tolerated in their youth activities or programs.
  - Have the members develop a statement which they can sign to confirm their support and which can be used publicly. The meeting should be limited to approximately one hour and should include an opportunity to ask questions.
  - Invite the press to attend the community meeting. Publicize it with a press release for local newspapers and newsletters.
- Enlist newspapers and newsletters to include coverage of community efforts to eliminate and prevent sexual harassment.
- Include sexual harassment information in materials about community youth activities that are distributed by the school and/or community groups to students and families.
- Invite community representatives to visit schools and observe programs on student-to-student sexual harassment.
- Promote the adoption of sexual harassment guidelines and materials for after-school extracurricular events and activities.
- Provide organizations sponsoring community youth programs with the same guidelines used by the school and classroom to ensure that students will receive a consistent message.
- Provide opportunities for community representatives to invite students to join program offerings such as clubs, sports, church and synagogue activities, bands, and orchestra. Outside activities and hobbies provide positive leadership skills, which help eliminate sexual harassment behaviors.
- Encourage all after-school personnel working in activities such as extended day programs, community clubs, family-run sports teams,

and church and synagogue youth activities to be aware of and to talk about sexual harassment to their groups.

- Share district materials on sexual harassment and allow them to be reprinted and used by community programs and organizations.
- Allow and encourage district staff who are knowledgeable about sexual harassment to address community programs and organizations.
- Continue an ongoing dialogue with community representatives. These meetings and activities need to be continuous and reinforced for positive results.

Keeping Written Records

Keeping records of harassment incidents, complaints, and retaliation is essential in documenting the frequency of harassment, describing the process of handling reports and complaints, providing a record of the school's actions, and helping to monitor the effectiveness of how complaints are handled. Should there be any legal proceedings, school records can be used to justify or criticize the school's handling of incidents.

Information should be reported in detail without any value judgments, opinions, speculations, or conjectures such as "This child looks like he is lying."

Districts should organize and develop their own reporting forms to include the information, listed in compliance with already-existing policy and procedures. Specific forms for reporting sexual harassment incidents and follow-up actions help staff follow required procedures and keep adequate records.

A form should be developed to describe the initial information for each incident, observed or reported, to be recorded by school personnel. The elements of a reporting form are outlined below. A separate file for each incident should be developed and include all written communications as well as memos of phone calls and descriptions of meetings and decisions. These records should be placed in a locked file with limited access.

SEXUAL HARASSMENT REPORTING FORMS

Description of Incident in Detail

Use a separate sheet for each incident where necessary and include:

- Who experienced the harassing behavior: Name(s) and grade
- Who was responsible for the harassment: Name(s) and grade
- Date and time incident was reported
- To whom was it reported
- Date and time incident occurred
- Where did it happen
- Who was involved
- Who saw it happen
- Source(s) of information for description of incident
- What happened (Use extra paper if needed)

Response to Incident

- Immediate response, if any, and by whom
- What, if any, additional response is needed, and by whom

Additional Information Needed

- Signature and title of person writing this report
- Date report was written

(The form should include directions to return it in a sealed envelope within twenty-four hours, with the name, title, address, phone, and e-mail of the person to whom it should be sent.)

Section to Be Filled Out by Administrator

Does the incident need to be reported to state and local authorities? (The form should summarize the types of incidents that must be reported according to state laws, State Department of Education regulations, and district policy, *even if* minors committed the act(s). In most states, for example, touching someone's genitals is a form of sexual abuse and must be reported by schools.)

[Note: Notification to appropriate state and local authorities does *not* relieve the district of its responsibilities to stop the harassing behavior.]

If the incident needs to be reported, include:

- Who was notified
- Date
- By whom
- How (phone, letter, mail, e-mail, other)

Notification of Incident to Students and Their Family

Was the family (families) of the harassed student(s) notified about the incident?

- Date
- By whom
- Which family member
- How (phone, letter, mail, e-mail, other)
- Response, if any

Was the family of the student who engaged in harassing behavior notified about the incident?

- Date
- By whom
- Which family member
- How (phone, letter, mail, e-mail, other)
- Response, if any

Resolution Procedures

- Date and who took each action should be listed. (Each meeting should be recorded separately.)
- Meeting(s) with student who was target of incident
  —Date, time, and place
  —Who was present
  —Description of meeting, including decisions made
  —Action, if necessary, to be taken: by whom and when
  —Follow-up when necessary, and by whom and when

Meeting(s) with accused student(s)

- Date, time, and place
- Who was present
- Description of meeting, including decisions made
- Action, when necessary: by whom; when
- Follow-up when necessary, and by whom

Meetings with other staff

- Date, time, and place
- Who was present
- Description of meeting, including decisions made
- Action, if any, to be taken: by whom and when
- Follow-up when necessary, and by whom

Additional Actions, If Any, by School Personnel, Including Teachers

Information about each action and by each individual should be recorded separately.

- Name(s) of staff responsible for carrying out each decision
- Name(s) of staff receiving written notification of actions to be taken
  —date
  —by whom
  —how (phone, letter, mail, e-mail, other)
  —response, if any
  —follow-up when necessary, and by whom
- Description of actions, if any, to be taken by student who was harassed
- Description of actions, if any, to be taken by accused student
- Description of other actions, including referral of students to outside agencies or other sources of help
  —description of action
  —by whom
  —date

Written Notification of Resolution to Be Sent to All
Students Involved in the Incident(s) and Their Families

Information should include a description of the incident(s) and steps taken to resolve the problem. The letter should encourage students and families to contact the school if they have any questions regarding the resolution. (Sample letters of resolution addressed to the student who was harassed and to their families and to the student who engaged in harassment are provided in chapter 6.)

Written Notification of Resolution to Student Who Was Harassed and to His or Her Family

- Date
- By whom
- Which family member
- How (phone, letter, mail, e-mail, other)
- Response
- Follow-up when necessary and by whom

Written Notification of Resolution to Student Who Harassed and to His or Her Family

- Date
- By whom
- Which family member
- How (phone, letter, mail, e-mail, other)
- Response
- Follow-up when necessary, and by whom

Follow Up with the Harassed Student
to Determine Whether Harassment Has
Stopped and Whether Any Retaliation Has Occurred

Determine if additional action is needed.

- Date
- By whom

- Conclusions
- Follow-up:
  — description of follow-up actions
  — name of the person(s) responsible for follow-up actions
  — was the follow-up completed?
  — if completed, when?
  — if completed, by whom?

Additional Information Needed

- Signature of person(s) who wrote the records
- Signature of administrator

Information on how records should be kept when investigations are conducted appears in appendix B in the section "Keeping Written Records of the Investigation."

Information on records of staff and student training appears in chapter 4.

WHAT TO INCLUDE IN DISTRICT ANNUAL REPORTS

An annual report for the district is important because it ensures that certain policies and continuing activities and programs are periodically evaluated for their effectiveness so that changes in policy and practice can be made if necessary. The report is helpful in monitoring how well a policy is working and assessing what kinds of training are needed, what information needs to be disseminated, and what can be done to improve the effectiveness of the antiharassment efforts.

The annual report should include, at a minimum:

- A summary of training activities
- A summary of dissemination activities
- A summary of the cases reported, including the number of cases resolved formally and informally. Names and other identifying information should be sanitized or omitted. Data should be reported by school, grade, race, *and* sex of harassers and victims, type of incident, and outcomes. Incidents of multiple harassment (such as

race and sex) should be reported separately. Descriptions of actual incidents and how they were handled, and what happened subsequently, help people understand what kinds of behaviors are prohibited and demonstrate how the district is taking an active role in ending these behaviors. Information such as the following should be included:

—a description of selected cases

—comparison with previous year(s) data

—problems encountered

—plans for coming year, and

—recommendations for improvements

The report (or a summary of it) should be disseminated to all administrators, staff, families, and the board of education. An abbreviated version could be distributed to older students as part of a training and dissemination program.

How to Investigate a Complaint of Sexual Harassment

Investigations are conducted when a student denies the accusation of sexual harassment and/or a formal complaint has been filed. If a student fully acknowledges that he or she engaged in the sexually harassing behavior, and there is no reason to believe that other students were harassed, there may not be any need for an investigation. In some instances the only purpose of an investigation will be to substantiate the student's admission, if needed. A report will still need to be written, a resolution of the incident implemented, and the penalty determined.

If a pattern of harassment is believed to have existed, an investigation may be necessary to implement a formal sanction and/or to ensure that the behavior does not recur. Districts should develop written investigative guidelines.

PROCEDURES

All formal complaints require an investigation when there is a disagreement about what happened. All steps of the investigation should be documented in writing.

It is *not* necessary for a formal complaint to be filed in order for a school to conduct an investigation; a district can initiate an investigation even without a complaint.

Investigative procedures should respect rights of all parties, including basic due process, and should be fair to all the individuals involved.

The procedures should apply equally to both students involved; that is, if one is allowed to bring an attorney to an investigation interview, the other should also be allowed to do so.

Before disciplinary action is taken as a result of a formal complaint, the student who is accused should be given timely and adequate notice in writing, describing the allegations, and an opportunity to respond to them before a neutral person or panel.

Persons investigating or making decisions should have no conflict of interest preventing them from acting fairly, such as having a personal or professional relationship with any of the students involved or their families.

Procedures should be timely—there should be time frames for each step of the investigation and subsequent actions. Investigations that are delayed in starting or take a long time to complete diminish trust in the procedures. Investigations should begin within a few days after the school has been informed about an incident and should be completed in approximately two weeks or less, if possible.

CONFIDENTIALITY

While never absolute, confidentiality should be honored to the extent possible by all staff who have knowledge of the incident(s) and subsequent actions taken by the district, the students involved, and their families. Some people believe that neither the student who complained nor the student who is accused or their families can be legally bound by the district's confidentiality policy; nevertheless, students and their families can be asked to observe it.

CONSULTATION WITH THE DISTRICT'S ATTORNEY

The district's attorney should be consulted when:

- The harassment is very serious, including touching, sexual abuse, sexual assault, and physical assault.
- The harassment continues, despite interventions.

- There are questions about legal issues.
- There is potential, attempted, or actual violence; threats; stalking; intimidations; sexual abuse; or sexual assault.
- The district is considering bringing its own complaint against one or more students.
- The district may be liable for teacher or administrator actions or inaction that failed to follow the district's policy.
- It appears that confidentiality has been breached.
- It appears likely that litigation may result.
- Either party engages an attorney.
- There are free speech issues.
- There are academic freedom issues.
- Multiple harassment is involved, such as harassment based on sex *and* race, national origin, or physical disability.
- A complaint is not timely or is otherwise rejected.
- Other information is needed before the investigating team can make its decision.
- There is a negotiated agreement.

The attorney should also be consulted before any written documents are finalized. These may include letters to the student who complained, the student(s) involved, their families, and witnesses and any written notification of disciplinary action. [Note: A copy of each formal complaint is routinely sent to counsel in some districts.]

CHARACTERISTICS OF A GOOD INVESTIGATOR

The success of an investigation is in part determined by the characteristics and knowledge of the investigator. A good investigator should:

- Have knowledge *and training* in issues dealing with sexual harassment, including understanding of relevant legal issues and the legal rights and responsibilities of all people involved
- Be familiar with the district's policies dealing with sexual harassment

- Be familiar with the district's organizational structure
- Have credibility within the district community
- Represent the district in a fair manner
- Be neutral and not reach a conclusion until the investigation is finished
- Maintain confidentiality
- Refrain from doing counseling with parties, and refer them elsewhere if counseling is needed
- Be sympathetic to all parties in a neutral manner
- Be nonjudgmental and nondefensive
- Have the ability to make tough decisions regarding truthfulness and credibility of students and witnesses
- Have the ability to make tough recommendations when someone has been found guilty of violating the policy
- Maintain complete written records of all information, interviews and determinations, and decisions
- Have the ability to work as part of a team
- Take immediate action when necessary, such as arranging to remove offensive materials or graffiti from a wall, or obtaining protection for someone who is being stalked.

DETERMINING WHETHER AN INVESTIGATION IS NECESSARY

Assess whether the complaint is amenable to informal resolution and whether the student who complained wants to attempt informal resolution. If informal resolution is being attempted, there may not be a need for an investigation, for example, if the student decides to write a letter to the harassing student and the harassment stops.

Assess whether the complaint is timely. The time for bringing forth a complaint of sexual harassment should be able to be extended for good reason, for example, if the student who complained was seriously ill was told by a teacher that the student ought to be able to handle it alone, or was threatened with retaliation by another student and therefore did not complain further at that time.

Even if the complaint is not timely the district may still take action, especially if there is reason to believe the complaint is valid.

- Someone in authority might speak to the student who was accused of harassing behavior. (For a description of how that conversation should be held, see the section on dealing with students named in anonymous complaints below.)
- The family of the accused student might be informed of the accusation.
- The teachers of the student who is accused might be informed and asked to be alert to sexual harassment by that student.
- There might be a discussion of the issue with the student who complained and his or her family to inform them about how the district is responding. If the family is notified about the incident, explain to the student why this is being done, if possible, before the family is notified.

Assess whether the complaint presents a sexual harassment issue. For example, "Almost every day he calls me a porcupine and says I have cooties" is not sexual harassment, but the district may still need to respond, although not necessarily under the required sexual harassment procedures.

Be careful in rejecting complaints for not being sexual harassment. Do not assume the person is "overly sensitive" or that the complaint is "frivolous." It is better to investigate when the complaint contains *any* information about behavior that can be considered sexual. [Note: In *Davis v. Monroe County Board of Education*, 1999, the U. S. Supreme Court ruled that educational institutions covered by Title IX are required to take steps to address complaints about student-to-student harassment *when the school has actual notice.* "Deliberate indifference" to such a complaint can expose the school to liability. (In contrast, when employees are harassed, employers who "know or *should have known*" that harassment was occurring are obligated to respond.)]

If the complaint is rejected:

- Write a report explaining why the complaint was rejected.
- Talk to the complaining student (and his or her family) about why the complaint was not accepted as a sexual harassment complaint,

what other options may exist, and what the school plans to do to handle the issue, if anything.

Assess whether the complaint is so serious (for example: sexual abuse, assault, or attempted assault; possibility of physical danger; stalking) *that the institution must intervene immediately,* even if there is no formal complaint or before a formal investigation. In such cases, families should be notified immediately and police notification may be mandatory.

If graffiti is involved, arrange to have it removed immediately after photographing it.

If a student website or e-mail is involved in the complaint, quickly request that the family remove the offending materials. Check that the materials have actually been removed.

RESPONDING TO ANONYMOUS COMPLAINTS

Determine what to do about anonymous complaints. To the extent possible, the district needs to respond to anonymous complaints.

If neither the victim nor the harasser can be identified from the complaint such as "One of the boys is calling the girls 'sluts' and 'whores,'" it is still possible take some action, such as:

- Remind teachers and others in a position to observe students about their obligations to intervene and report such behaviors.
- Assess whether additional training is needed for everyone or for targeted groups such as a particular class, or staff group, such as lunchroom monitors.
- Publicize the incident if the individuals involved cannot readily be identified. The incident could be described in the school newspaper, during an assembly, over the public address system, or in a memo to each class to remind students that such behavior violates the school's policy, that students are encouraged to report such behavior, that the school will protect the confidentiality of the persons who report such incidents as much as possible, and that students will be protected from retaliation.

If an anonymous complaint includes information that can lead to identification of an individual or pattern of behavior, as in "One of the guys in our Advanced Algebra class is snapping girls' bras and making sexual comments," it may be possible, with a little searching, to identify the class and the teacher. In such a case action should be taken, such as talking to the student engaging in the sexually harassing behavior; working with the teacher to handle the behavior; and/or providing training specifically for that class, which includes the reported behavior as an example of behaviors that are prohibited.

If the harasser is named in an anonymous complaint, the school is in a position to respond differently, although it still might implement some of the actions listed above. (If a school has been informed about someone who has possibly engaged in sexually harassing behaviors, the district could be liable under Title IX if it intentionally ignores the complaint. Just as important, not doing anything will undermine trust in the school's ability to handle sexual harassment. If there is no intervention, the harassment is likely to increase as well as be extended to other victims.)

In all instances involving anonymous complaints, the school should investigate to assess what action is needed. If the information is not conclusive, rather than doing nothing, schools may find it useful, in some instances, to inform the student who is accused in the anonymous complaint that he or she was accused anonymously, *offering it as information and not as an accusation.*

- Ask the student why he or she thinks someone complained about him or her.
- Remind the student that such behavior, if it did occur, violates the school's policy.
- A summary of the policy might also be given to a student who is in middle or high school.

Talking to the student is important because:

- It may stop the behavior.
- It may protect the district from liability because it responded to stop the behavior.

- If the complaint is false, it alerts the accused student to be more cautious.

Anonymous information *by itself* cannot be a cause for discipline. However, single or cumulative anonymous information about a particular situation or individual may be enough to trigger additional actions such as an investigation.

PLANNING THE STRATEGY FOR THE INVESTIGATION

- Add the name of the student who complained and the student who is accused to the master file list. A master file is essential to tracking all complaints. The file could identify a student who harasses often or has harassed in other schools and ought to be treated differently from a first-time offender.
- Set up a new confidential file for this case if this has not already been done. Include copies of all relevant *current* policies, including those that might also cover sexual harassment, such as an honor code. It is important to include these policies in case of legal action, which may take years to adjudicate and during which time the policy may have changed.
- Develop a list of those who have access to this file, such as the principal and vice principal and support staff who may be handling the file. Inform each person, including support staff, about the confidentiality requirements. They should not discuss the case with anyone and they should not keep the file on their desk when it is not in use. This warning could be incorporated into a letter which informs these persons about the complaint.
- Inform the district's attorney about the charge and the investigation.
- Identify other parties who need to know about the complaint and the investigation, such as the teachers of the student who was harassed and the student accused. Remind them about the following:
  - confidentiality: Only those with a need to know should be informed.
  - retaliation: They should know how to respond and whom to contact immediately if they observe or learn of retaliation or new incidents of sexual harassment.

- Identify issues that need to be decided.
- Identify witnesses who need to be interviewed.
- Identify documents that need to be obtained.
- Prepare a list of general questions for each interview. Many questions or a sequence of questions are likely to be repeated for some or all of the witnesses.
- Identify someone to notify the accused student about the complaint if not already done, including giving the student a copy of the complaint and asking him or her to avoid any unnecessary contact with the complainant. Inform the accused student about the prohibition of retaliation, including examples of retaliation.
- Inform the student who was harassed about the policy prohibiting retaliation, give examples, and ask her or him to report it immediately should it occur.
- Depending on the nature of the complaint and the comfort level of the student who complained, there may need to be a temporary seating, class, or school reassignment of the accused student to reduce contact between both students.
- Set up a time line, including those items that have time frames for completion as set by the district policy on sexual harassment:
  - when interviews will be conducted
  - when notes for each interview will be transcribed and typed, and by whom
  - when the investigation process will be completed
  - when a decision will be made as to what the investigation found
  - when actions, including disciplinary procedures, will be taken, if an investigation concludes that harassment has occurred
  - when parties and others with a need to know will be notified
- Allocate responsibilities. Often several people are involved in parts of the investigative process, such as the district's attorney, the person doing the investigation, the superintendent, the principal, and support staff.
  - Who is the lead person for the specific investigation?
  - Who will set up appointments?
  - Who will interview and who will take notes at each interview?
  - Who will arrange for interview rooms?
  - Who will maintain the records?

- —Who will inform those who need to be informed both before and after the investigation?
- —Who will communicate with the district's attorney and top administrators when needed?
- —Who will monitor the time line to see if it is on time or to make adjustments?
- —Who will talk about confidentiality to support person(s) who will be involved with the confidential files?

- Ensure that everyone involved in the process has no bias or conflict of interest (such as a personal or professional relationship with any of the students involved or their families).
- Ensure that everyone understands what must be kept confidential.
- Ensure that everyone understands they are not to talk to the press. Everyone involved in the process should know who is the staff member who will talk to the press about what is happening. It should not be anyone dealing directly with the investigation.
- Determine who will review the records of interviews and make the final decision. The policy should indicate who makes the decision as to whether the policy was violated, for example, the person conducting the investigation, the principal, or the superintendent.
- Determine who will write the final report of the investigation.

What to do if the student who complained also files a charge against the school with the U.S. Department of Education Office for Civil Rights or a state agency or goes to court? The fact that someone filed a complaint elsewhere is not a reason to stop the investigation. To do so might be considered as retaliation. In some instances, the satisfactory resolution of a complaint might lead to the withdrawal of charges filed by the target of harassment.

KEEPING WRITTEN RECORDS OF THE INVESTIGATION

Remember that all records are confidential. Nevertheless, keep in mind that records could become public as part of a future legal proceeding or in response to freedom-of-information requests under state public documents laws. Lists of questions that team members ask the district's attorney may be protected and therefore need not appear in the confidential file.

Records should reflect what the investigators find out, *not* conjectures or speculations. "During the interview he tapped his hands and blinked excessively"—*not* "He looks like he isn't telling the truth." Describe the *behaviors* of the person being interviewed, rather than your feelings or opinions about the behaviors.

Record nonverbal behavior, such as inappropriate laughing or gestures that contradict the spoken word. Record specific behaviors that suggest that the person may have been under the influence of substances that might affect recall, judgment, or the ability to comprehend questions.

Inform the person who types the records and/or maintains the files about the need for confidentiality. Try to have only one person maintain the files.

Write up records of all interviews and all contacts with the student who complained, the student who is accused, and all witnesses, within a day or so. Some interviewers ask the person interviewed to review the notes and sign that they are accurate.

For additional information on record keeping, see appendix A.

HOW TO CONDUCT AN INTERVIEW

Interviews can be tape-recorded if the person being interviewed agrees.

Both the student who complained and the student who is accused should be allowed to bring someone with them. A family member should be allowed to accompany their child, but should be advised not to participate in the interview. Similarly, an adult witness should be allowed to bring another adult with them but should be informed that that person will not be allowed to participate directly in the investigation. However, they can communicate with the witness at any time. If they start to participate in the interview, they should be reprimanded and informed that if it happens again they will have to leave. If possible, try to seat the family member in back of the student and out of the student's line of sight, so that he or she is less likely to influence how the student responds. Do the same for an adult accompanying an adult witness.

If the policy allows attorneys to be present, they should be informed prior to the interview that they will not be allowed to participate directly in the investigation but can communicate with their client at any time. If they start to participate in the interview, they should be reprimanded and informed that if it happens again they will have to leave. If possible, try to seat the attorney in back of the student and out of the student's line of sight, so that the attorney is less likely to influence how the student responds.

If possible, one member of a two-person team should ask the questions and the other should take notes.

All students and adults involved in the incident(s) should be interviewed separately. Persons interviewed separately are more likely to tell their own story rather than support someone else's. The interview should be conducted in a private setting, with the door closed.

Allow sufficient time for each meeting, at least one hour.

Develop, in advance, a list of questions:

- Names of alleged harasser and student who complained
- Relationship of student who complained to the student who is accused
- Relationship of person being interviewed to the student who complained
- Relationship of person being interviewed to the student who is accused
- Details of the alleged misconduct, including date and time, place, circumstances, and witnesses
- Effect of the alleged harassment on the student who complained
- Response to the incident by the student who complained before and after filing the complaint
- Reaction of the accused student to the complaint

Ask each of the students involved how they would like to see the incident resolved, if possible, such as "What do you want to happen next?" This can often be helpful in working out the actual resolution, as well as providing an opportunity to explain what is possible or not possible under the policy.

Be aware that the experience of being interviewed is stressful and may lead to anxiety and to defensiveness.

COMMENTS AND QUESTIONS
APPROPRIATE FOR ALL INTERVIEWS

- Thank the student or adult for coming, at the beginning and at the end of the interview.
- Explain that you will be taking notes (or using a tape recorder) to be sure you get all the information down accurately.
- Explain the process of investigation in a supportive manner. Seek the person's cooperation.
- Ask the person if there are any questions he or she would like to ask about the procedure before questioning begins.
- Reassure the person that all information will be kept confidential to the extent possible and that no retaliation will be permitted.
- Be sympathetic in a neutral manner such as, "This is hard to talk about," "I know this is difficult for you."
- Do not be afraid to be silent after you have asked a question or if the person is upset. You can give them some reassurance ("I'm sorry this is hard for you") and then wait silently for them to be ready to talk again.
- Give all parties the opportunity to ask questions. Record the questions asked and try to answer in ways that communicate the fact that the institution takes sexual harassment very seriously.

Witnesses may ask who suggested their name and why they are being asked to testify, and want more information about the incident. It is better not to relate who suggested their names. Tell them in a neutral manner that there is reason to believe that they may have information that would be helpful to the investigation. Explain that all the information you have and the information given to you is confidential and will only be shared with those who have a need to know. If witnesses do not want to testify, inform them in a factual manner that you will have to note their participation was requested and that they refused to cooperate.

Both the students involved and other witnesses should be asked if there is anyone they would suggest to be interviewed because they might have knowledge of the incidents or other relevant information. Witnesses can include students, teachers, other staff, volunteers, and visitors. (However, character witnesses are not appropriate for school sexual harassment investigations.) Sometimes there are no witnesses.

Persons with information about the complaint include:

- Those who observed or might have observed the incident(s) or have knowledge of it
- Those who were told about it by the complainant
- Those who observed the victim's reactions or changes in behavior by either party

Ask if there is anything else the person would like to add or whether they have any questions. Those being interviewed should also be asked if there are any documents that might be helpful, such as journals, calendar entries, or notes.

INTERVIEWING THE STUDENT WHO COMPLAINED

- Recognize that it may be difficult for the student to talk about what happened.
- Use open-ended, non-leading, nonjudgmental questions, such as "What happened?" "Tell me more," rather than "Why were you wearing such skimpy clothing?"
- Do not ask questions about prior or current sexual conduct or activities of the complainant.
- After asking about the incident(s), ask how the student felt about the incident(s), both when they happened and afterwards.
- Ask the student if there are any documents such as journals, calendar entries, or notes, or if anyone they know has information about the complaint, including:
  —anyone who observed or might have observed the incidents or have knowledge of them
  —anyone whom the student told about the incident
  —anyone who observed the student's reactions or changes in behavior
- Ask if there is anything else the person would like to add.
- Reassure the student again that you will maintain confidentiality to the extent possible and that retaliation will not be permitted.

- Give some examples of retaliation and ask the student to report them to you or other persons in authority should there be any retaliation during or after the investigation.
- Ask how the student would like to have the matter resolved, but do not promise any specific results.
- Ask if the student has any additional questions.
- Inform the student about how long the investigation is likely to take, without committing yourself to a rigid time schedule.
- Inform the student that he or she will be notified about the decision.
- Thank the student for coming.

INTERVIEWING THE STUDENT WHO IS ACCUSED

- Assure the student that he or she will have an opportunity to talk about what happened.
- Be aware that accusations of wrongdoing, whether accurate or not, may lead to anxiety and to defensiveness.
- Use open-ended, non-leading, nonjudgmental questions, such as "What happened?" "Tell me more," or "Why did you do that?" rather than "Why would you do such a stupid thing?"
- Do not share statements by witnesses with the student who is accused, although you will want to review the material they contain with the student.
- Give the accused student the opportunity to comment on the accusations.
- If the student denies the allegations, ask the student why he or she thinks the complaint was filed.
- After questions have been asked about the incidents, ask if there are any documents such as journals, calendar entries, or notes, or if there is anyone who has information about the complaint, including:
  - those who observed or might have observed the incidents or have knowledge of them
  - those who were told about it by the complainant
  - those who observed the other student's reactions or changes in behavior by either student

- Ask if there is anything else the person would like to add.
- Reassure the student again that you will maintain confidentiality to the extent possible and that retaliation against him or her or against the student who complained will not be permitted.
- Give some examples of retaliation and ask him or her to report to you or other persons in authority should there be any retaliation during or after the investigation.
- Ask if the student has any additional questions.
- Inform the student about how long the investigation is likely to take, without committing yourself to a rigid time schedule.
- Inform the student that he or she will be notified about the decision.
- Thank the student again for coming.

AFTER THE INVESTIGATION

Reaching a Conclusion

There are four possibilities concerning a determination:

1. The harassment occurred.
2. The harassment did not occur.
3. The allegation was unsubstantiated but had probable cause. (Many districts do not allow this as a possible decision.)
4. There is not enough information to make a determination. (This does not mean that the harassment did not occur or that the complaint was false.)

Weighing the Evidence

The criterion for weighing evidence is **not** "beyond a reasonable doubt." That is the appropriate standard for a criminal trial but not for an administrative proceeding in an educational institution. The standard is "the preponderance of evidence," that is, given the preponderance of evidence, a reasonable person would conclude that this occurred (or did not occur).

- All evidence should be weighed, including factual evidence by witnesses, observations of their conduct, and circumstantial evidence that supports or negates their statements or has bearing on the truthfulness of a witness.

- When reviewing all interview notes and materials, make a list of unanswered questions or information that needs clarification.
- Make a list of all verifiable facts that would substantiate the claim, and see whether they can be verified.
- Obtain additional needed information if possible.
- Make a list of the facts relevant to the complaint that must be true for the allegation to be supported. List the supporting data for each fact that has been obtained.
- Evidence presented by a person of authority such as an administrator or supervisor should be given no more credibility than evidence from a student or lower-level employee.

Assessing Credibility

A decision can be made that harassment occurred even if there were no witnesses to the harassment when the evidence of the complaint is credible. The following can be helpful in assessing credibility:

- Changes in the behavior of the complaining student resulting from the harassment would add credibility. For example, after being harassed, the student cried, was upset, avoided class or certain areas; his or her grades dropped, etc. However, if none of these things occurred it would not mean that the complaint was not credible, only that the student who complained was affected differently or less intensely.
- The harassing behavior continuing after the student was informed that the behavior was unwelcome would add credibility.
- Major inconsistencies in testimony would detract from credibility.
- A delay in reporting the harassment does not detract from credibility because many students delay reporting because of fear of retaliation, not knowing or trusting the policy, fear of being blamed for causing the harassment, not understanding it was harassment, etc.
- Documents such as diaries, calendar entries, journals, notes, or letters describing the incident(s) would add to credibility.
- Other complaints against the accused would add to credibility.

- The fact that a relationship was at one time consensual does not detract from credibility nor is it a defense against a charge of sexual harassment. Consensual relationships can be followed by sexual harassment when one person tries to end the relationship and the other person uses his or her "power" to intimidate the former partner into staying in the relationship.
- The fact that the alleged harasser *did not intend* to harass the complainant is not a defense to a charge of sexual harassment. It is the *act* itself that is important, *not the intent* of the person who engaged in the behavior.
- Not knowing that the behavior was offensive and unwelcome is not a defense to a complaint of sexual harassment.
- The fact that the student who filed the complaint did not tell the alleged harasser that his or her behavior was offensive does not affect credibility. Many students are afraid of doing so. Additionally, there is no obligation for the complaining student to inform the alleged harasser that his or her behavior is offensive.
- Motivation to lie, exaggerate, or distort information should be assessed when there are differences in what was reported.
- Questions to consider in assessing credibility:
  - How might a reasonable person react to the incident(s)?
  - What was the effect of the behavior on the complainant?
- Explanations of why the harassment occurred do not add to credibility. Students who have sexually harassed other students often acknowledge their behavior but explain and defend it in ways that do not justify their actions and should not add to their credibility. To the contrary, such "excuses" should be seen as admissions of having engaged in sexually harassing behaviors.
  - It was an accident—I didn't do it on purpose (from a student who put his hands on a female student's crotch).
  - I didn't know it was against the rules.
  - I was just joking around.
  - I was just playing when I grabbed his penis.
  - She flirts all the time.
  - I was just flirting with her.
  - She was asking for it—look at what she's wearing!
  - You have to understand, we guys have special needs.
  - It's no big deal. I don't know why she is so upset.

—I wasn't lying. She really is a slut (bitch, whore, etc.).
—She's a snitch for telling on me.
—We just wanted to teach him a lesson about being a fag.

The following do not add to or detract from credibility of the accused student:

- Character witnesses (He is such a good kid; I know he would never do that.)
- Popularity with staff and other students (Everybody likes him; I just don't believe he would do that.)
- A history of no past problems (He's never been in trouble before.)

The following do not add to or detract from credibility of the student who brought the complaint:

- Clothing (Just look at what she was wearing.) Clothing does not cause sexual harassment, nor does it give anyone permission to touch or make sexual remarks.
- Appearance (She is so pretty no wonder he did it.) (She is so unattractive! I don't believe anyone would do that to her.)
- Flirting behavior (She's always flirting with the boys, what did she expect?)
- Males being victims (He should have realized she meant it as a compliment.)
- Sexual orientation of victim (Listen, he came out of the closet and told everyone, he should have expected that people would act like this.)
- Athletic participation and concern about the team or "getting a good student in trouble"

DETERMINING THE PENALTY
WHEN THE POLICY HAS BEEN VIOLATED

The policy should describe the various penalty options, such as:

- Prohibition from participation in all extracurricular activities
- Prohibition from attending graduation

- Saturday detention or after-school detention
- Transfer to another class or school
- Suspension
- Expulsion

In addition to the punishments listed above, a student who violated the policy may be prohibited from speaking to the student who brought the complaint.

[Note: Although referral to counseling or out-of-school therapy may be useful, it should never be considered as "punishment."]

WRITING A REPORT ON THE FINDINGS

The report should include the following information:

- Introductory data: complainant's name, accused's name, type of complaint, date filed, name of person and office that received complaint, and name(s) of investigator(s)
- Background information: the history of the relationship between the parties and other details surrounding the complaint
- Summary of the complaint: the specific allegations
- Findings from the investigation concerning each allegation
- Conclusions: whether or not sexual harassment occurred
- Recommendations for corrective action if the conclusion is that sexual harassment occurred
- Right to appeal, if any, including name of person to whom the appeal is addressed, time limit for appeal, and conditions of appeal
- Signature of investigator(s) and date of report

AFTER THE REPORT IS WRITTEN

Who Gets a Copy of the Report?

Person(s) originally notified about the complaint (such as the principal and vice principal) should receive the report (or a summary). Include instructions that it not be duplicated or shared with anyone without a need to know, and that it should be kept out of view.

It is useful to have a central confidential repository of complaints and findings.

Should the report be given to complainant and alleged harasser? Policies vary: some people say yes, some say no, some allow it to be read but not copied, some allow a written summary. At a minimum both students need to be informed orally about the findings of the report.

Meeting with Involved Students

Meet separately with the student who complained and the student who was accused. (Try to see both within the same day if possible.) Share the findings and whether the complaint was substantiated or not, and what happens next.

In meeting with the accused student:

- If the complaint is unsubstantiated warn the student that if there are subsequent charges this complaint might be given weight against him or her.
- If the decision is inconclusive, state that serious allegations were made and if similar allegations are made in the future, appropriate action will be taken.
- Reiterate prohibition against retaliation to *both* students:
  —Include examples.
  —Encourage the complainant to report any examples of retaliation from anyone on campus.
  —Encourage both students to meet with you or other staff if they want to talk about what happened or about other issues.
  —Provide both students with sexual harassment materials (such as a brochure) if this has not been done already.
  —Explain appeal procedure, if any.

WHAT ELSE NEEDS TO BE DONE

If the complaint has been publicized, the institution may make a public statement about the resolution, informing both complainant and alleged harasser beforehand. The names of students should not be revealed in the statement, even when in some instances the names are already known by many students.

The teachers of *both* students should be informed of the outcome and be instructed to watch for further harassment or retaliation (from any students) and instructed how to respond and to whom it should be reported. The victim should be observed to assess whether any additional help is needed.

MAKING THE HARASSED STUDENT WHOLE

Regardless of the findings, steps might be taken to help the student who brought the complaint.

- Counseling. At the conclusion of the complaint process, the harassed student should be reminded that counseling is available.
- Protection against retaliation. A follow-up with the harassed student to see that there is no harassment should be made shortly after the incident occurs, a week or so after the complaint process is finished, and about a month later. This could be in the form of a note, phone call, or e-mail or with a direct contact with the student.
- Training of staff and/or students. It is helpful to hold sexual harassment workshops, particularly with those in the unit where the harassment occurred. For example, depending on the nature of the harassment and where it occurred, the students in a particular class might receive some additional information or a workshop about sexual harassment; bus drivers might receive additional training on how to intervene or report harassing behavior; or teachers in a particular grade might receive intervention training.

After a finding of harassment and if the harasser is not transferred to another school, the school will want to make an arrangement so that contact between the two students is minimized, such as assigning them to different classes where possible. If there is no other alternative and both must attend the same class, the teacher should be informed to keep the students apart, such as not assigning them to the same small group or assigning them to sit next to each other. The teacher should also be reminded to intervene and report any behaviors that appear to be sexual harassment or retaliation.

The student who brought the complaint should be moved only if he or she is agreeable to do so and requests it. Under no circumstances should the student who complained be pressured to move to another classroom, school, or activity. Moving the student who complained but not the student who was harassing often sparks a controversy because students, families, teachers, and other staff may perceive the harasser as not being punished and the victim as being reprimanded.

What if a student wants to drop out of school before, during, or after an investigation or attend another school? Occasionally during an investigation, especially when expulsion and/or criminal charges are possible, the family of the accused student may pull the child out of the school before the investigation is finished, often just as a punishment is being decided. In such instances, the student and the family should be told that a letter will be placed in the student's records stating that the student transferred out of the school while a complaint of sexual harassment of another student was pending (or after he or she was found guilty). If the student who was accused of harassment leaves before the investigation is completed, inform the student who complained and his or her family.

If the student who filed the complaint wants to transfer to another school or leave the district school system at any time during the complaint and during the investigatory process, it is important to talk to the student and/or the family to establish whether retaliation has occurred or if there are any misunderstandings or failures on the part of the complaint and investigatory process. However, if the student and family feel that a transfer is best for the student's well-being, the transfer should be facilitated.

As with all contacts, document any interviews, phone calls, and e-mails with students who complain, students who are accused, and their families.

A Brief History of
Student-to-Student Harassment

1964: Title VII of the Civil Rights Act of 1964 is enacted. It prohibits discrimination in employment on the basis of race, color, national origin, religion, and sex. Educational institutions are largely excluded from its coverage until it is amended in 1972.

1972: Title IX of the Education Amendments of 1972 is enacted. It prohibits discrimination on the basis of sex in all federally assisted programs. It covers students, faculty, staff, and the entire institution in all of its activities if it receives *any* federal dollars.

1974–1975: The term *sexual harassment* is first used by Lin Farley and others at Cornell University to apply to workplace harassment.

Mid-1970s: The first cases involving sexual harassment in the workplace wend their way through the courts, which are asked to decide whether sexual harassment is a form of sex discrimination. These cases typically focus on a woman whose supervisor pressures her for sexual activity. Initially, the courts do not consider sexual harassment as a form of sex discrimination.

Mid-1970s: Faculty harassment of students at the college level begins to emerge as an issue.

1976: First federal case (*Williams v. Saxbe*) to hold that sexual harassment in the workplace is a form of sexual harassment.

1977: First charges of sexual harassment against an educational institution are filed under Title IX when Yale University is sued by five students charging faculty with sexual harassment of students.

1979: First national report on campus sexual harassment of students by professors is published by Bernice R. Sandler at the Association of American Colleges and Universities. Student-to-student sexual harassment is not mentioned.

1979: The U.S. Supreme Court rules that individuals have a right to sue under Title IX even though the statute did not explicitly provide for such action.

1980–1981: First study on peer sexual harassment in high schools is conducted by Nan Stein for the Massachusetts Department of Education.

1988: First national report documenting college student-to-student peer sexual harassment by Jean O'Gorman Hughes and Bernice R. Sandler is published by the Association of American Colleges and Universities.

1989: Minnesota passes first law requiring every school in the state to develop and post a policy of sexual harassment.

Late 1980s/early 1990s: First cases of student-to-student sexual harassment emerge in colleges, high schools, and elementary schools.

Early 1990s: Computer sexual harassment cases begin to emerge where students send harassing messages to others and where students put pornography on school computers, sometimes as part of the log-in process. Issues of free speech begin to be raised as a defense against sexual harassment.

1991: The Minnesota Human Rights Commission approves a settlement of $15,000 between the Duluth School District and the family of a girl about whom vulgar graffiti had been written on the walls of the boys' bathroom. May be the first case in which monetary damages are awarded in a student-to-student sexual harassment case.

1992: The U.S. Supreme Court rules unanimously in *Franklin v. Gwinnett County Schools* that students who experience sex discrimination, including sexual harassment, can seek monetary damages from their schools and school officials under Title IX.

1993: The Office for Civil Rights at the U.S. Department of Education rules that an Eden Prairie, Minnesota, school district violated Title IX when it allowed a hostile sexual environment to continue on a school bus. A first-grade girl filed charges when kindergarten-to-fourth-grade boys continually made lewd and intimidating statements to girls.

1993: The first national survey of sexual harassment (*Hostile Hallways*) in the nation's elementary and secondary schools is published by the American Association of University Women. The study, conducted by Lou Harris and Associates, found that 85 percent of girls and 75 percent of boys experienced some form of sexual harassment at school. Only 7 percent told a teacher and 23 percent told a parent or family member. One in four girls reported being harassed by a teacher or school employee.

1993: The Minnesota State Board of Education becomes the first to approve a curriculum dealing with sexual harassment, including peer harassment, for students from kindergarten through high school.

1994: The Office for Civil Rights of the U.S. Department of Education rules that sexual graffiti must be removed because it violates Title IX.

1995–1998: Courts disagree as to whether schools are liable under Title IX for student-to-student sexual harassment.

1996: Sexual harassment of female athletes by male athletes begins to emerge. A University of Nebraska committee finds that male athletes often intimidated and harassed female athletes. Three female student athletes sue Temple University, claiming that male athletes regularly engaged in suggestive, sexually offensive, and lewd remarks, gestures, and behaviors.

1996: California court awards $500,000 to a female student (Tianna Ugarte) after finding that she had endured months of sexual harassment from a sixth-grade classmate, including sexually obscene gestures, name-calling, and violent threats and that the Antioch (Calif.) Unified School District had ignored her complaints. The case is finally settled for $450,000.

1996: The U.S. Supreme Court refuses to review *Rowinsky v. Bryant Independent School District* in which the appellate court had ruled that the school was not liable for student-to-student harassment in which eighth-grade boys had touched the breasts and genitals of two sisters. The appellate court said that schools would be liable only if they handled claims of sexual harassment differently for boys and girls.

1996: The U.S. Court of Appeals for the Seventh Circuit found in *Nobozny v. Podlesny* that a school system was liable under the Fourteenth Amendment right of equal protection for not having stopped harassment based on the sexual orientation of a former student while he was in middle school and high school. The school system agreed to pay the student $900,000.

1997: Petaluma School District in northern California agrees to pay $250,000 to a former student who had endured taunts and sexual references from other students while she attended junior high school from 1990 to 1992.

1997: The Office for Civil Rights of the U.S. Department of Education issues (March 13, 1997) its "Sexual Harassment Guidance: Harassment of Students by School Employees, Other Students, or Third Parties" describing compliance standards under Title IX for campus and school policies on sexual harassment. The "Guidance" makes it clear that institutions are responsible for student-to-student harassment and details the standards that the OCR will use and that institutions should use as they investigate and resolve allegations of sexual harassment of students engaged in by school employees, other students, or third parties.

1998: In a Title IX case involving a teacher who seduced and harassed a student (*Gebser v. Lago Vista Independent School District*), the U.S. Supreme Court rules that a student may not sue a school district for a teacher's sexual harassment unless a school official with authority to institute corrective measures knew about the teacher's misconduct and the school acted with "deliberate indifference" by failing to take effective steps to stop the harassment. (This means that the standards for holding schools liable for sexual harassment of students are stricter than those required for employers being held liable for sexual harassment of employees.)

1998: Shortly after the above decision Richard W. Riley, secretary of the U.S. Department of Education, issues a statement noting that the court's decision in *Gebser* explicitly recognized that the department can do the following:

> enforce administratively its Title IX regulation that requires schools and school systems to have well-publicized policies

against discrimination based on sex, including sexual harassment discrimination; to have effective and well-publicized procedures for students and their families to raise and resolve issues; and to take prompt and effective action to equitably resolve sexual harassment complaints. (Press release, July 1, 1998)

1999: In *Davis v. Monroe County Board of Education*, the U.S. Supreme Court rules on May 24, 1999, that under Title IX schools are obligated to take steps to address complaints about student-to-student sexual harassment. The case involved a fifth-grade girl who was harassed by a boy in her classroom. He repeatedly tried to grab her breasts and other parts of her body and made vulgar comments to her. The classroom teacher took no action, even refusing for three months to allow the girl to change her seat. The principal also took no action even though the child's mother complained after each incident. The girl's grades dropped and she wrote a suicide note.

Under the court's decision, schools that are "deliberately indifferent" when they have actual notice of sexual harassment can be held liable. The majority decision makes it clear that mere teasing or bullying would not subject schools to liability under Title IX, and holds that harassment must be severe, pervasive, and objectively offensive, such that it deprives the victims of access to the benefits of education.

The decision puts colleges and school districts on notice to take student-to-student sexual harassment seriously and to intervene when students' learning environment is affected; for example, educational institutions should establish guidelines, inform their school community about them, and respond to students' calls for help.

2001: The Office for Civil Rights of the U.S. Department of Education issues (March 13, 1997) its "Revised Sexual Harassment Guidance: Harassment of Students by School Employees, Other Students, or Third Parties," revising its 1997 "Guidance" in light of subsequent Supreme Court decisions. The "Revised Guidance" reaffirms the compliance standards that the Office for Civil Rights applied in investigations and administrative enforcement of Title

IX, as well as distinguishing them from the standards applicable to private litigation for money damages. In most other respects the "Revised Guidance" is identical to the 1997 guidance.

2005: In *Jackson v. Birmingham Board of Education*, No. 02-1672, the U.S. Supreme Court rules on March 29, 2005, that Title IX prohibits schools from retaliating against those who bring sex discrimination complaints, including third parties who complain about sex discrimination on behalf of others.

Jackson, a male high school teacher, was fired from his position as coach of the girls' basketball team after he complained about inequities experienced by his team as compared to the boys' team. For example, the girls' team had a smaller budget, had no ice available for injuries, and played in a nonregulation gym.

The decision puts colleges and schools on notice that anyone who reports sex discrimination (including sexual harassment) is protected against retaliation even if the person did not directly experience the discrimination.

(Excerpted and updated from "Important Events in the History of Sexual Harassment in Education," by Bernice Sandler, in *About Women on Campus*, newsletter of the National Association for Women in Education [now defunct], Spring 1994, pp. 5–6.)

Selected Resources

Aronson, E. *Nobody Left to Hate: Teaching Compassion after Columbine.* New York, W. H. Freeman, 2000.

Describes the "jigsaw classroom," a type of cooperative learning; how it is used to improve relationships among black, Hispanic, and white students; and how to defuse the exclusionary practices of cliques. Although not intended to cover sexually harassing behaviors, many of the strategies included encourage cooperation and thus are likely to decrease peer sexual harassment. See website: www.jigsaw.org

Beane, A. L. *Bully-Free Classroom: Over 100 Tips and Strategies for Teachers K–8.* Minneapolis, Minn.: Free Spirit Publishing, Inc., 1999.

Provides strategies for teachers to use in dealing with bullying; many are useful for sexual harassment incidents.

Borkowski, J. W., L. A. Brown, J. A. Dodge, N. Gittins, J. W. Jacobs, G. Jaffe, N. F. Krent, R. W. Schwartz, and M. Sneed. *Student-to-Student Sexual Harassment: A Legal Guide for Schools, Revised Edition.* Alexandria, Va: National School Boards Association Council of School Attorneys, 2000.

Describes legal issues and others such as policy development, investigations, and training. Contains reprints of some government documents.

Conn, K. *Bullying and Harassment: A Legal Guide for Educators.* Alexandria, Va.: Association for Supervision and Curriculum Development, 2004.

Examines various legal issues, such as civil rights and free speech protection under the Constitution; legal definition of harassment based on gender, race, religion, and disability; computer bullying and harassment; and threats of violence against classmates and schools.

Fineran, S. "Adolescents at Work: Gender Issues and Sexual Harassment." *Violence against Women* 8, 8 (2002): 953–67.

Explores the little-examined area of high school students experiencing sexual harassment while working part-time. The study raises the issue of what schools should do to help teens protect themselves and for schools to be aware of how on-the-job harassment can affect students' self-esteem, identity formation, and school behavior.

Fineran, S. "Sexual Harassment between Same-Sex Peers: Intersection of Mental Health, Homophobia, and Sexual Violence in Schools." *Social Work* 47, 1 (2002): 65–74.

Provides a historical and legal framework for peer harassment and explores mental health implications for both boys and girls. Contains recommendations for schools and for social work practice concerning peer sexual harassment in schools.

Harassment-Free Hallways: How to Stop Sexual Harassment in Schools. Washington, D.C.: American Association of University Women, Educational Foundation Sexual Harassment Task Force, 2002; updated in 2004.

Provides materials including sample policies and resources for students, parents, and teachers. Can be downloaded in PDF format at www.aauw.org/ef/harass/index.cfm

Hostile Hallways: The AAUW Survey on Sexual Harassment in America's Schools. Washington, D.C.: American Association of University Women, Educational Foundation, 1993.

Reports the results of the first national study on student-to-student harassment in public schools, grades 8–11. Unlike many studies, this survey included Hispanic, white, and African American students. See website: www.aauw.org

Hostile Hallways: Bullying, Teasing and Sexual Harassment in School. Washington, D.C.: American Association of University Women, Educational Foundation, 2001.

Updates the information from the 1993 survey. See website: www.aauw.org

Human Rights Watch. *Hatred in the Hallways: Violence and Discrimination against Lesbian, Gay, Bisexual and Transgender Students in US Schools.* New York: Author, 2001.

A comprehensive look at the experience of lesbian, gay, bisexual, and transgender students, teachers, and administrators; the impact of these experiences; what needs to be done by schools; and legal standards.

Jones, R. " 'I Don't Feel Safe Here Anymore': Your Legal Duty to Protect Gay Kids from Harassment." *National School Board Journal* 186, 11 (1999): 26–31.

Describes examples of harassment of gay students and the legal reasons for schools to become involved. Can be viewed at www.asbj.com/199911/1199coverstory.html

Langelan, M. *Back Off! How to Confront and Stop Sexual Harassment and Harassers*. New York, Simon & Schuster, 1992.

Discusses harassment in general and focuses primarily on adults, but the author also interviewed students who were harassed. Relates successful strategies used by these students.

Mullin-Rindler, N. *Relational Aggression and Bullying: It's More Than Just a Girl Thing*. Wellesley, Ma.: Wellesley Centers for Women, Wellesley College, 2003.

Disputes the hypothesis that girls' "meanness" to other girls is new and unique to girls and explores it as part of a larger pattern of societal violence. Includes school strategies.

Mullin-Rindler, N. *Selected Bibliography of Children's Books about Teasing and Bullying for Grades K–8, Revised and Expanded Edition*. Wellesley, Ma.: Wellesley Centers for Women, Wellesley College, 2003.

Contains several hundred listings of children's literature, classroom and Internet resources, and references for teachers and parents. Although the materials focus on bullying and teasing they will be helpful to students with sexual harassment issues.

Permuth, S. *A Legal Memorandum: The Internet, Student's Rights and Today's Principal*. Reston, Va.: National Association of Secondary School Principals, December 1998.

Describes legal issues concerning the Internet, students' rights, and censorship, and includes a sample policy of acceptable use of school computers.

Revised Sexual Harassment Guidance: Harassment of Students by School Employees, Other Students or Third Parties, Title IX. Office for Civil Rights, U.S. Department of Education, January 19, 2001.

Replaces the March 13, 1997, *Sexual Harassment Guidance* in limited respects in light of recent Supreme Court cases relating to sexual harassment in schools. The document has been archived and can be found at www.ed.gov/offices/OCR/archives/shguide/index.html [Note: The 1997

Guidance is still posted on the OCR website; the newer and current definitive *Guidance* is available only in the archives. OCR will not provide a written copy of the current guidance even though it is still in effect. Anyone needing a copy of the current guidance and without access to the web should write their senator or representative and ask them to obtain a written copy.]

Rich, D., and H. Stonehill. *MegaSkills Essentials Source Book*. Washington, D.C.: Home and School Institute, 1993–2000.

A resource book that accompanies training for teachers, administrators, and counselors. Provides a full curriculum, integrations, adaptations, and school–family connections for direct use with students K–8. Materials focus on reading and developing the attributes necessary for academic achievement and character development—attributes necessary in the prevention of sexual harassment.

Rich, D., and H. Stonehill. *MegaSkills Leader Training for Parent Involvement*. Washington, D.C.: Home and School Institute (available in Spanish), 1987–2001.

A resource book that accompanies training for teachers, administrators, counselors, and community leaders. The book provides eleven workshops for leader use with families. Age-coded activities are provided for parents to use with their children. These activities focus on literacy and developing the positive attributes necessary for learning and self-discipline behaviors necessary in preventing sexual harassment.

Rich, D., and H. Stonehill. *MegaSkills Parent Handbook/English/Spanish*. Washington, D.C.: Home and School Institute, 1992.

Provides activities for families to use with their children at home K–4. The activities, written in both English and Spanish, focus on literacy and the development of attributes necessary for learning and positive behaviors.

Russo, H. *Young Women with Disabilities*. National Coalition for Sex Equity in Education. *NCSEE News* 98–99, 4 (1999): 19–20.

(NCSEE has changed its name to the Association for Gender Equity Leadership in Education.) Website: www.agele.org

Sandler, B. R., and M. Paludi. *Educator's Guide to Controlling Sexual Harassment*. Washington, D.C.: Thompson Publishing Co., 1993.

A comprehensive looseleaf notebook updated monthly and covering most aspects of sexual harassment in K–12 and colleges and universities. Includes material on policies, practices, and legal issues.

Shakeshaft, C. *Educator Sexual Misconduct: A Synthesis of Existing Literature*. U.S. Department of Education. Retrieved July 22, 2004, from www.ed.gov/rschstat/research/pubs/misconductreview/report.pdf

Provides a comprehensive examination of sexual misconduct by teachers and staff. Recommendations for schools include training and education of students about this issue, which could be incorporated into existing programs.

Shakeshaft, C., L. Mandel, Y. M. Johnson, J. Sawyer, M. A. Hergenrother, and E. Barber. "Boys Call Me Cow." *Educational Leadership* 5, 2 (1993): 22–25.

Discusses the results of a student-to-student harassment survey representing low-income, middle-class, and wealthy families in middle and high schools in Long Island, N.Y. The study describes forms of harassment experienced by students, who were most likely to be harassed, whether the harassment was reported, and what happens when it was reported.

Shoop, R. J. *Sexual Exploitation in Schools: How to Spot It and Stop It*. Thousand Oaks, Calif.: Corwin Press, 2004.

A reference for those interested in teacher or staff sexual exploitation of students.

Shoop, R. J., and J. W. Haybow Jr. *Sexual Harassment in Our Schools: What Teachers and Parents Need to Know to Spot It and Stop It*. Boston: Allyn and Bacon, 1994.

Provides suggested policies, procedures, and programs for use by parents and schools.

Stein, N., and L. Sjostrom. *Flirting or Hurting? A Teacher's Guide on Student-to-Student Harassment in Schools (Grades 6 through 12)*. Wellesley, Mass.: Wellesley College Center for Research on Women, 1994.

Provides practical strategies and programs for preventing sexual harassment.

Strauss, S., with P. Espeland. *Sexual Harassment and Teens: A Program for Positive Change*. Minneapolis, Minn.: Free Spirit Publishing, 1992.

Strengthening the Learning Environment: A School Employee's Guide to Gay and Lesbian Issues. Washington, D.C.: National Education Association, 1999.

A useful handbook for school employees.

Tune In to Your Rights: A Guide for Teenagers for Turning Off Sexual Harassment. Ann Arbor: University of Michigan, 1985.

A booklet discussing sexual harassment and what students can do about it. Available in English, Spanish, and Arabic.

Williams, V., and D. Blake. *Do the Right Thing: Understanding, Addressing and Preventing Sexual Harassment in Schools. A Practical Guide for Educators, Parents and Students*. Washington, D.C.: National Women's Law Center, 1998.

Discusses what schools should do when sexual harassment occurs, how to prevent it, what victims can do, and how to ensure fairness to persons accused of sexual harassment.

WEBSITES

Though almost all of the sites dealing with bullying prevention do not mention student-to-student sexual harassment, many of the strategies and programs suggested to prevent bullying are useful to prevent peer sexual harassment. In addition to those already listed, the following may be helpful.

www.bullyfreeworld.com Lists research and strategies used in the United Kingdom.

www.bullying.co.uk Lists policies and programs in the United Kingdom.

www.glsen.org Website for the Gay, Lesbian, and Straight Education Network for parents, students, and educators. Contains a variety of information, strategies and resources.

www.nyu.edu/education/metrocenter/EAC/resource.html Contains an annotated bibliography of books and articles about K–12 peer sexual harassment.

www.titleix.info Sponsored by the National Women's Law Center. Contains information about a wide variety of issues and strategies relating to Title IX, including sexual harassment.

About the Authors

Bernice Resnick Sandler, EdD, is a senior scholar at the Washington-based Women's Research and Education Institute, where she consults extensively with institutions and others about sexual harassment and discrimination against women and girls. She has given over 2,500 presentations, written extensively about women's equity, and served as an expert witness in discrimination and sexual harassment cases. The *New York Times* called her the "godmother of Title IX" for her work in the development and passage of Title IX. Sandler was responsible for the first national reports on campus sexual harassment, peer harassment, gang rape, and the chilly classroom climate. She also consulted with The Citadel on its "female assimilation plan." Often quoted in major media, she has appeared on numerous national and local talk shows. Her work has been extensively quoted and included in Supreme Court briefs, and she has been honored with numerous awards, including ten honorary doctorates.

Sandler wrote (with Lisa A. Silverberg and Roberta M. Hall) *The Chilly Classroom Climate: A Guide to Improve the Education of Women*; edited (with Robert J. Shoop) *Sexual Harassment on Campus: A Guide for Administrators, Faculty, and Students*; and was the major author of *Educator's Guide to Controlling Sexual Harassment*. Her website is at www.bernicesandler.com

Harriett M. Stonehill, MS Ed, is an educator and administrator who serves as director of the MegaSkills Education Center, Home and School Institute in Washington, D.C. The Institute focuses on the educational and character development roles of schools, family, and community to further the academic achievement of students. During the past fifteen years she has traveled to over 250 cities and has trained over 6,000 MegaSkills leaders in 48 states, involving community organizations, corporations, and educators. She has coauthored, with Dorothy Rich, the *MegaSkills Leader Training Handbook for Parent Workshops*; *MegaSkills Essentials for the Classroom*; *Professional Development Curriculum Handbook*; *New MegaSkills Bond Connections Handbook*, a comprehensive training program to build teacher/parent/student partnerships; and *MegaSkills Parent Handbook*, an English and bilingual handbook for families to use with their children. She also serves as editor of the MegaSkills Leader Workshop Program publications.

She is a noted speaker both nationally and internationally, and contributor to professional journals. Prior to her work at the Home and School Institute, Stonehill served as teacher, as staff to the White House Conference on Families, and as a public interest advocate for legislation on education and employment for major national organizations.